# ALTITUDE
## Tales of Resilience

by
K. Fitz

> If you purchased this book without a cover you should be aware that this book is stolen property. It was reported as "unsold and destroyed" to the publisher, and neither the author nor the publisher has received any payment for this "stripped book."

**ISBN:** 978-0-578-42743-0

**Altitude**

Copyright © 2018 by Kenneth Coleman

All rights reserved. This book or parts thereof may not be reproduced in any form, stored in any retrieval system, or transmitted in any form by any means—electronic, mechanical, photocopy, recording, or otherwise—without prior written permission of the publisher, except as provided by United States of America copyright law.

This is a work of fiction. Names, characters, places, and incidents either are the products of the author's imagination or are used fictitiously. Any resemblance to actual persons, living or dead, businesses, companies, events, or locales is entirely coincidental.

For permission requests, please contact the author via the "Contact" page on the following website: www.officialkfitz.com

**Proudly self-published through Divine Legacy Publishing**, www.divinelegacypublishing.com

In Loving Memory of
Douglas Ray Bridgers (Daddy)

I never truly knew my father growing up. And I was so caught up in wondering what happened to him that I didn't realize that my daddy was standing in front of me for 29 years. You are still my inspiration and set the bar for how a man should carry himself. I'm so happy to be in this moment writing this work. This book is in dedication to you and everything you stood for. You stood for power, strength, love, compassion, audacity, and fatherhood.

(Shooby-Dooby)

# Acknowledgements

I can't believe this book is finally done. It took forever to make this happen. I know where to begin, but I don't know where to go after that. I'll just let my hands to the typing and the soul do the thanking.

My Lord and Savior, Jesus Christ, thank you for giving me the mentality to get this book done. You know that I spent late nights wondering if I could even get this book done. But You told me to give myself a date and a consequence if I failed. And I did and I came out on top and completed it on time.

My beautiful wife, Markitta. You and I have been to hell and back with our children, our marriage, our degrees, and our careers. But we figured it out, pulled off our MBAs, and got a book done in the middle of it. I'd have to say that you and I are some mad mofos. Seriously, thanks for standing by me when I was more than ready to self-destruct. When I felt like the world was against me, you stood by me. That can't be taken for granted and has to be screamed on the loudest stages. Thank you. We will celebrate with a bottle of sparkling water and get back to raising these little ones.

My Grandmother, Joann. You are my sunshine in a room full of darkness. I know that you have only meant the best for me throughout my life. You have been a rock and performed incredibly since Dad left us, and you will continue to do so. I love you and will have your back until the day you join him. You are a Queen and carry your crown and pearls very well. I love you Mommy dearest!

My kids: Hadessah, Gabriel, and Catherine. You three have been the spark that has made this book happen. To be honest, I hope this book sells. Because if it does, BAM!!!! There's your tuition. All jokes aside, you kids have been a blessing and are unlike any other children on this Earth. Especially you, Hadessah, my oldest. Thank you being my Kid Leader and making sure your brother and sister were taken care. I know you wish you could've gone outside to play sometimes, you three. But I couldn't watch because daddy was writing this. When you're older, you'll see this and understand why I did what I had to do.

Valerie. Thank you for the late night talks when I thought was going to lose my mind. Thank you for never judging me. In fact, I can't say you've ever intentionally judged me with the intent of finding something wrong with me. That's to be respected and honored. I am blessed and most appreciative to be your son-in-law.

Will Murry. In the words of The Usos, we are on that "Day One Ish". We've been grinding day in and day out to have moments that we can both celebrate. Find time to celebrate for me this week. The Black Tie Group now has a book!!! Ric Flair voice: WOO!

Erinn Marks. Sister, you have been a rock in my life when school became Hell. You've coached me on life beyond the Army and served as a mentor at a time in my life where I needed someone to mentor me rather than hurt me. Thank you for holding it down. The future is bright.

James Hawes. Brother, it's been a ride hasn't it? From the day I met you, I knew you were a special guy. You personified genuineness, commitment, love, and conviction to develop your fellow man. I finished this book with you in mind. In fact, you're in one of these chapters somewhere. I've already forgotten which one, though. I appreciate you and your unconquerable soul. Cheers!

Donnell. When I was a young man, you believed in my talent. You believed in the boy who was just a dancer at Reid Street Community Center and saw celebrity potential in me. You drove me to auditions, allowed me to record music in your office area, and took me to church on Sundays when I was trying to find my way back to God. If you didn't save another soul on this Earth, you saved mine. Thank you.

Deonta, DJ, Darius, and Danyale. What a ride this year has been, right? But we've still got each other. We are still alive and carrying his name high on our backs and daring anyone to come check us, right? At the end of the day, we are family and are undoubtedly here for one another. Let's keep it that way.

GLEMBA 19 to include Pam, Rhonda, and Connie. This is special for me. I was able to pull this off while in this MBA program based on life experiences and from observing many of you. Everyone in our MBA program is a future C-Suite Executive. I just know it! Thank you for being awesome classmates and allowing me to learn from each of you one slide, one discussion board, and one International Retreat at a time! #WHOOSH #UTD #GLEMBA

Mike Saul. Sir, you gave me the idea in the first place to write this book. I had zero intentions of writing a book until you gave me the idea. Now I'm sitting here 9 months later after our conversation with a finished product. You are a true mentor committed to building better men. The final chapter is for you, my friend. Thank you.

Joe Bowman. Thanks for being the best military mentor I've ever had. Thanks for trying to warn me before I walked in to the fire. Luckily everything worked out to my good, as I knew it would. You are a leader and I look forward to hearing of your future moves. Thanks for being the greatest.

You. Thanks for buying a copy of this book. I desire to give you the realist content possible. I hope this is a blessing to you and you close this book with tools (new and old) that help you evolve and grow even bigger than you already are as a person.

# Author's Note

I poured my heart in to this book. This book is a hybrid of self-help and fictional storytelling with auto-biographical information. The stories I tell you about me are all 100% real. I will not redact the stories to try and make myself look like a cooler or better guy. This is who I am, and I'm not ashamed of it. I wanted to make sure you received raw content that matters. I want you to walk away thinking a few different things:

1.  Wow, this guy can write.

2.  Wow, this is a good a%^ book!

3.  Wow, this guy has been through some things.

4.  This is a book that I could pass along to (insert person's name). They would really benefit     from this.

So, this book is about a guy named Ken and his buddy Lex who formed a team of hikers to climb Mount Altitude. As they climb, their lives change forever.

The idea for this book was presented to me by a good friend of mine named Mike. I told him about some of my life experiences and he made it clear to me that these stories and life events needed to be given to the world to teach others where to capitalize and when to walk away. This book didn't become a serious deal to me until the passing of my grandfather.

When he passed, something snapped inside of me, and I became obsessed with getting this book out to the world. I wanted to tell his story and mine. I wanted a document that could build leaders and give lessons learned that could change lives forever. That's exactly what this book is intended to do and at the conclusion of reading this book, your thoughts will change. Your mind will think differently. And you will seek to go to the next level in Altitude. So, I am not going to build some super long prologue for you. Besides, most people skip the prologue and go straight to Chapter One anyway.

Enjoy the book and be inspired.

Oh yeah, lastly, don't forget to check out the Altitude Podcast on major podcasting platforms (Apple Podcast, Google Play, PocketCast, etc).

# Chapter One: Accept Your Purpose

Drivers who drive while drunk have a higher likelihood of dying in an accident or killing others while behind the wheel. The same is for the purpose in your life. If you steer the course impaired by misinformation and an unclear course, you're likely to cause a collision and casualties. Everyone is here with a purpose regardless of the size of their dream or vision. However, it's amazing how much wasted potential arrives within and leaves this Earth. You have to clear the path or expect substandard or negative results.

If you don't like the course you're traveling, then change your moves. Adjust how you execute your moves if you are genuinely committed to going to a higher altitude. If you're doing something, including reading this book, just so you can feel good about yourself, then you're wasting your time and the energy that the universe is blessing you with. I'll let you in on a secret:

---

*If you were called to be a visionary, the LEAST you can do is provide a "vision".*

---

It almost sounds rude and disrespectful for me to lay it out to you like that, right? Well, GOOD! I want the message to burn some people. Because there are people who know they've been called to a higher altitude in life and are unwilling to do their part to fulfill their destiny.

The most irritating part about it is that there are people who wished they had half the knowledge on subjects you've mastered. There are people who wished they had the financial ability to make minor investments in their future so they could benefit from wise spending. There are even people who wish they could just be in the presence of the people who encourage others. You have every tool that they'd kill for and some of you are out here blowing through these resources like they are a birthright. You were only born with two birthrights: **life and death.**

Now, I have my philosophy based on my personal experiences that can assist with your thought process. But hey, at the end of the day, only you can envision and make the decision for you. Everyone around you just talks. It's your responsibility to create a vision. So check these out and let's see where your mind goes. Here are some questions for you to answer before we really dig into actions:

1. Are you waking up in the middle of the night after dreaming about a life you wish you lived?
2. Are you waking up from dreams envisioning how your lifestyle will be if you don't chase your dreams?
3. Can you write down everything that you expect yourself to have on a piece of paper along with why you deserve it?
4. What pride will you get from accepting your purpose?

5. Is the dream really yours or are you envying someone else?

**Accept That You Have a Purpose**

Read this carefully and internalize what I'm about to tell you. Your purpose in life was pre-determined before you got here. However, you are given free will. Freewill gave you the choice of either fulfilling your purpose or not, the same way it gave you the option of where to place your faith.

---

*"You intended to harm me, but God intended it for good to accomplish what is now being done, the saving of many lives." -Genesis 50:20*

---

This means that as you walk the road towards your purpose, everything that comes that we perceive to be damaging and painful was meant to complete your story of glory. You can't be afraid to accept that there is a purpose for you.

Have you ever watched a movie where an oracle tells the king that someone is going to rise up and attempt to take over his kingdom? In some of those movies, the king walks around in fear and makes no moves but to build up their defenses against what's coming. Then there are kings that know the inevitable danger coming their way, lace up their boots, assemble their army, and go to war accepting that they may not come back. I said that to propose this question to you….What type of king or queen do you want to be? **You will be able**

**to look back on your life and figure out which kind of kingdom mentality you promoted.**

There are plenty of people in this world who are terrified to accept that they are meant for a greater purpose. Not everyone is meant to drop a record, make a hit, and pull up in a fancy car within 24 hours. Some of us are designed to stand before the masses touching lives through our unique contributions. Your gifts are going to point to your purpose. Now let me make this very clear: there is a difference between gifts and skills. Skill is what pays the bills; a gift is what you're passionate about and can generate your vision through. Skills point out man-made things that you have learned over time. Now, don't get me wrong. Skills aren't a bad thing. In fact, I promote acquiring as many skills and certifications as possible to increase the likelihood of achieving the top of the mountain. But you know when you were given a gift.

**Assassinate the Fear**

My good friend, Will, told me a quote from the late-great Dick Gregory, may he rest in peace. "Fear and God do not reside in the same place." If you walk around in a spirit of fear and timidness, then expect to never reach the destiny. In order to step into that fold, you have to be ready to come out of your fear and do what you were meant to do.

This might mean that you will have to risk being laughed at. You may be ridiculed. You may be embarrassed if a project fails. That's okay. It's better to have peace in knowing that you truly reached for the stars. Isn't it interesting that so many people want to be at the very top but are unwilling to take the risk involved with being the #1 guy? To take the risk involves stepping out on faith and a willingness to try. You know the number one place the majority of the human race decides to perform reflection? **ON THEIR DEATHBED**, sadly enough. On the deathbed, people reflect on beautiful memories and how good their lives were. But eventually, that dangerous two-word question pops its ugly head up for many unfulfilled people…What if?

A gift enters your presence when man-capable talent meets God-given purpose. Dr. Myles Munroe made the point of saying, "People will pay you to fulfill your purpose". I know you may want to be the starting quarterback for that team on your wall, but that may or may not be for you. You may be meant to do something else. The lawyer, analyst, or coach for that team in the future. And if so, it's okay. I know it doesn't sound like it right now, but you have to trust that it is. There's always a reason that the chips fall where they do based on our contributions to influencing what happens. You've got to understand that…

---

*"Many are the plans in a man's heart but the Lord's purpose for a man will prevail." - Proverbs 19-21.*

---

You may even achieve your dream right before God decides to activate His purpose in your life. Not to mention you may pay for not answering the mail when destiny calls for you. The universe has a weird way of aligning to bring order as directed by the highest power. Let me give you a personal experience to bring this home. The book you are reading right now, the company I created, and work that I continue to build were built by a being much higher than me. I can't take credit for this. This company was put in my heart, mind, veins, ribs, soul… ALL OF THAT!!!!! But before I realized this vision, I had some other goals in mind.

At the age of 27, I was a United States Army officer desperate to do something big with my life. I had just finished working at an Armor Brigade on Fort Bliss, TX. I knew my next move was to become a Commander. I had already been offered multiple opportunities internal to the Brigade. I was so excited that I couldn't wait to take on the new challenge. But, during a major exercise, I bumped into a commander who was external to the Brigade who eventually offered me a command position. Although I wanted to take the job, I knew that this particular unit wasn't where I belonged. However, I felt that taking the unit he offered me would improve my likelihood of getting promoted. However, I had already made the decision to resign my commission in the Army at this point.

To another soldier, the wisest decision would have been to assume command while serving in the Armored Brigade and resign commission once the goal was completed. However, greed and the desire to look even better when I got out the military resulted in me taking that command. So what were the results of my performance while in that position? This leadership position was the first crash and burn in my life. It concluded in a poor evaluation report that depicted me as a wild child who was rude, disrespectful to others, and didn't shine a light on the performer I knew I was. I believe to this day if I would've taken command at one of the other units, this wouldn't have been a problem.

I veered off the path that God was clearly preparing for me to seek out dreams and visions that weren't meant for me. However, like I've already said, the universe will continue to align our movements as directed by God. After my tragic command time, I was re-stationed at Fort Sam Houston and put in a position to slow down my life and reset myself. I took time to reflect on my life. Some of those moments were positive and some were miserable. There were so many days of wondering if I was achieving my purpose. It also forced me to think on something that I had been running from for a while: my relationship with the military.

I wanted to get out of the military back in 2012 when I realized I wasn't having fun anymore. I had dreams of leaving the military and starting up a company of my own or becoming a high ranking executive. However, fear crept in and my perspective changed. I kept repeating the same questions that most soldiers failed to answer when they decided to leave the military before retirement age:

- Do you have a plan?
- What are you going to do when you get out?
- You know you got a family, right?
- So you're going to go and chase a dream that could possibly fail and leave you sitting around looking stupid?

Now to those who have never been in the military, it almost seems like common sense right? Ummm, yeah I can make it on the real world as a civilian. People do it every single day. But I've got to speak from a soldier's perspective. When you are about to walk away from a guaranteed check, where only you can only be fired by making poor decisions, and you receive benefits that civilians are fighting to have, the decision becomes a little more challenging.

Then, on top of those questions, there are other senior leaders in the military telling those guys that are thinking about getting out:

- You only have to stay in 5-10 more years, and after that, you've got a paycheck for life.
- You have free medical care, man.
- You're practically guaranteed to be promoted every so often.
- You can leave the military; I'm gonna get this money.

I found myself feeling like a prisoner to other people's fears because I had ambitions and I wasn't happy settling on the military. I also found myself conversing with people about making the military my career, knowing that I had no intent of lasting another two years. In fact, a few of the guys I confided in about getting out of the military weren't happy being in themselves. That brought me to this question that messed my emotions up:

---

*"Why am I expressing my feelings, passion, and drive to people who don't have any?"*

---

I'm all for seeking counsel, which we will discuss later, but don't seek sadness unless you desire more of it. You have to be willing to step up in order to reach the next altitude. When the reports others provide don't make sense with what you believe is right, crunch them yourself. It took traumatic incidents from losing loved ones and career failures for me to move on to the next chapter in my life and that I needed to commit.

I wasn't going to be allotted another year to get it together. Either get it done now or I risked my calling to be given to someone who would heed the call and act. I finally accepted and located my purpose and it was sitting right outside of my "safety zone". I made the decision that, after 10 years of honorable service to the United States Armed Forces, it was time to go.

Why? It wasn't because I didn't love the military. It was because I had a different calling that was placed on my life from birth and, damnit, I knew it. If I chose to stay in the military, I would've lived in day-to-day mediocrity. A lack of desire plus subpar action will always equal mediocre results. Besides, we need the best, brightest, and most passionate leaders as we head into war. I had an avalanche-worth of passion, but it just wasn't for the Army any more.

When the day finally came that I locked in and committed to my purpose, my life changed forever. I started waking up with a purpose. Everything that I was doing around me had a goal attached to it. When I woke up in the morning, I began listening to entrepreneur blogs. My daily consumption even improved. Just including larger helpings of greens caused me to lose weight and improved my cognitive thinking. I planned my exercise regimen thoroughly. There was no more going to the gym just to go walk on a treadmill and leave. When I got to work, I focused on developing a new relationship with one person every day. While working, I focused on how to effectively manage my time to get results and build the team.

All these goals may seem like regular everyday tasks, but I saw them as, what I call, "preparation for my destiny". To be a good executive, you have to build a solid, daily routine with non-negotiable rituals. You have to eat to live; not just to taste. You have to be able to think, plan, and lead if you want to get to the next level in altitude. As I started to apply these small things, my thought process began to shift. My resiliency began to grow and my desire to create the most "locked-in" version of myself was within reach. But none of this would've ever happened if I didn't assassinate my fears. You have to think, plan, and execute your rituals daily if you want to get to the next level in altitude. All of these require confidence and discipline. But confidence and discipline don't arrive until fear departs.

**Man Makes the Title. Title Doesn't Make the Man.**

Titles should be used to define one's position, responsibility, and authority in an organization. It should not serve as your get out of jail free card or be used to make others do "as you wish, sire". There are a lot of people who want to grow and move higher in altitude but lack a drive to do it.. One of the reasons they can't go higher is the inability to be faithful over a few.

---

*"...you have been faithful over a few things, I will make you ruler*

*over many things." - Matthew 25:23*

---

If money is the root of all evil, then titles are often the branches on the tree. Keeping it as candid as possible, let me ask you a few questions:

- Why would I give you a million dollars, when you can't manage a thousand?
- Why should I finance you a Phantom when you can't maintain payments and maintenance Chrysler 300?
- Why should I give you a mortgage for a house when can't pay rent on your apartment?
- Why would you expect to become a world champion when you didn't put in the hours to become one?

The same thing works in leadership and purpose. Don't expect more when you can't handle less. It's not bad that you can't handle more yet. This is growth time. Embrace and capitalize on the opportunity to grow. But don't move up just to be called "boss" when you only possess "entry-level" performance potential right now. Stop asking for more when you can't even work with what you got. Master what's in your possession in order to reach the next altitude.

---

*If you're going to ask the universe to test you, the least you can do is complete the pre-requisite courses.*

---

If you're chasing titles, you'll never be happy. Once you finally achieve it, there won't be a higher altitude for you to climb. You can reach CEO, chairman, and owner and not be able to go higher. You can ALWAYS go higher when your life is tied to a meaningful purpose. You can ALWAYS go from helping 1,000 people to 10,000 people. You can ALWAYS go from thinking about you in the now to them in the future. Contributing to the greatness of others is a never-ending journey of servitude that pays off on a daily basis.

To take it up to the next level of honesty, here's another truth. ***Not everyone gets the mega titles.*** Everyone isn't going to be the President, Chief of Staff, lead guy, etc. Somebody has got to be the second-in-command or lower. I've seen so many people stab each other in the back over evaluations in aspiration to be promoted. Let me tell you right now, if it takes you destroying someone else through deceptive and demeaning methods, that's not purpose-driven work. Purpose-driven work is done with the faith that your work will produce the results that will open the predetermined doors.

Your purpose isn't in a title. Titles are superficial. Your purpose is in the contributions that you could give others once you've achieved a title or a body of work.

### "Why" Are You Doing This?

Purpose always goes back to the immortal question - "Why?" Why are you trying to reach the next level? Why do you want to be a CEO? Because the title sounds good? Or do you want to be a CEO because you can influence the company in a way that changes the world? One answer is based on life-changing principles and the other is based on the desire to acquire a tagline. Make sure your purpose is grounded with a clear reason.

I'm a firm believer that when doors open in your life, you must be ready. In addition to that, you must be ready for what's on the other side of that door. However, here's the truth: you'll never be 100% ready for what's coming. If your intentions are grounded with a true purpose, your commitment will always render you victorious. That means you have to have a reason "why" you're getting up and completing your daily rituals.

I've heard this question, "Why are you doing this?" so many times in different live speaker sessions and read it in many books. I'm convinced that if you can answer this question with a truthful answer, your gas tank will never go empty and you will be infinitely driven. Knowing how to answer the question of why you do what you do is critical. That answer is why you get up everyday with energy. That answer is why you commit an extra 15 minutes in the gym when everyone else leaves. It's why you wake up every day obsessed with just…being…greater.

If a situation comes and you weren't equipped for it, that moment was still meant to happen in your life; you were just meant to learn a lesson so you can win later. Everybody loves a good underdog story or song right? Let's use my come up anthem "Started from the Bottom" by Drake. In the song, Drake talks about struggling and achieving unbelievable greatness.

> *"Started from the bottom now, we here"* -Drake

We all love to hear that part of the song, right? What's funny is that many people are deaf to the parts of the song where the artist lays out the groundwork it took to get there. Never forget that why you're doing this is why you will continue to do it. Don't be afraid to evolve with your environment but evolve with a mission in mind.

**Why Some People Never See Their Purpose**

What if Steve Jobs died with the iPhone incarcerated in his mind? What if Martin Luther King, Jr. decided to ignore his beliefs and never stand up for civil rights? Inventions and rights we all get to share today could reside in coffins sealed away forever. The thought of wasted potential makes me upset and sick. I have a hard time accepting that people have died and taken dreams that could help mold our dreams with them. What if their tombstones read their true purpose?

- *Here lies the physician who could've invented the cure for cancer.*
- *Here lies the lady who was supposed to end world hunger.*
- *Here lies the mother who was supposed to birth a future President of the United States.*

There is no time limit for when you should begin your journey to your designed greatness. Balamurali Ambati was the youngest doctor in history at the age of 17 years old.

# Altitude

*When it comes to human potential, people who say the timing isn't right probably had their watches broken by fear, doubt, and insecurities.*

Some people never make it to their destination because they are too busy trying to live the same journey as someone else. Your assignment in life is different from those people to the left and right of you. You may cross paths; your paths may even be parallel. But they will never coincide. False purpose may save some souls; but you may lose yours in the process.

*Use other people's successes to help you develop benchmarks; not expectations.*

Growing up, I had a friend named Robert who inspired me so much. He was very intelligent, had both his mother and father in his life, and was an athlete in school. I felt like this guy's life was the life I wanted. Not to mention, he had a pool table in his room, the best games, and a cool mountain bike.

I felt cool just hanging around him. But as time passed, things began to change and I started to find myself. I started to realize that I wasn't being me when I was around him. I was being fake. I was being who I thought he wanted me to be in hopes of being accepted and appreciated by him and the guys he hung with. Eventually, I found out that I was going in the wrong direction and that I needed to branch away from him to develop me and find out who I was. I'm sure if I didn't separate and try to find myself, I'd still be lost until this day trying to become a version of "Robert". By the way Rob, if you're reading this book, I'm proud of you, brother.

Some people never reach their goals because of their family. Some families are unable to recognize gifts in their kids resulting in uncultivated potential; thus leaving the unlocking to the child or someone else. If the child is malleable and easily-influenced, this could lead to other issues. From another perspective, some family members live through their kids. The parents are so focused on living through their kids that the parents' vision automatically becomes the child's mission to achieve. This can lead to long-term issues. Your decisions can turn a human being into a robot.

Neighborhoods impact some kid's successes and, in this case, failures. In my city, the drug dealers made more money than my dad. So it was hard for me at times to be at school with some of the dealers who wore better clothes, rode in fancier cars, and had the baddest women. In hopes to make the same money, people join the drug game not knowing the possibilities once you're in:

- You get out clean.
- You die over turf.
- You go to jail and exponentialize the challenge of achieving your dreams.
- You get in the game and you can't get out.

There are plenty of other reasons why people never make it out. But what I will tell you is if you've got your hands on this book, you control your destiny. You own your purpose. Not your mom, dad, friend, wife, pastor, NO ONE ELSE BUT YOU. No one owes you anything and the excuses of why you haven't achieved your goals are irrelevant. God orders your footsteps; all you've got to do is follow the sequence. Get your mind right, lock-in, and #earnyourspot.

# DOPE Exercise 1: The Blurry Vision Test

*Where there is no vision, the people perish: but he that keepeth the law, happy is he. - Proverbs 29:18 KJV*

Okay now, it's time for a DOPE Exercise. DOPE is an acronym that stands for "Dream On Purpose Everyday". This is my exercise for you to do daily to provide you with reflection tools that you can utilize to gain more clarity in our discussed areas of your life. There will be at least one DOPE Exercise in every chapter that you can use as part of your daily reflection time as you see fit. I only have two rules for these: Trust the process and go the whole way. You aren't going to receive perfection by reading 5 pages. But if you apply the 5 pages, you will see results.

Not every vision comes to us clearly. And if it does, you're one step closer. But that doesn't excuse us from making an effort on our end to clear the fog. Today, you're your own optometrist. With that said, let's start off by testing your sight and identifying what your blurry vision looks like.

Take out a pen and three (4) sheets of paper. With only the first sheet of paper, I want you to answer this question, providing as much detail as humanly possible:

*What does your dream look like?*

I really want you to put some effort into answering the question. Get detailed and make it as big as you want. Write down what you do should be doing for a living, who you know, name some tangible items you own (houses, cars), and more. Write what makes you happy and any other emotions you want to feel. Go as deep and be as vulnerable as you can.

Now on the other page, I want you to write what your life is right now comparing based on what you wrote on the previous page. After you've finished, compare both side by side. HIGHLIGHT JUST WHAT YOU DON'T LIKE FIRST; then celebrate what you love.

Now, here's where I'm going to challenge you. On Page 3, I want you to write clear goals with dates that align with your life's vision… but based on what you've written on both lists. What many people will find out is that their ultimate vision doesn't align with their goals because their too small or irrelevant to their cause. If it's a "nice to have" goal, take it off the list. That's not a goal; that's just a desire. If you achieve your goals, your desires should be the results.

Once you've delineated your goals, use Page 4 to create your final goal list. With that final list, I ask you to do two important things for me: be ruthless in completing them and only share them with the ones you trust.

# Chapter Two: Prepare for the Climb

Before the big climb began, I gathered all 20 of the brave men and women coming with me. I held the meeting at 7pm to give everyone time to eat their meals and rest. But our dinner meeting didn't start until 7:20 because a few climbers showed up late. At that point, everything inspirational I had to say was out the window. But, my message didn't come off as... inspirational as I thought. In fact, it came off abrasive, but honest.

I remember saying, "Why do I even have you here?! You can't even show up on time to a sit down! Can I trust you to show up on time tomorrow to begin the climb? Can I trust you to have our backs if you're not even disciplined enough to be in place when we need you? Is someone going to die because you can't arrive on time? I tell you what. Leave...LEAVE!" But they didn't.

We identified the mountain that we wanted to climb. Now was the time for everyone to understand this would not be an easy feat for anybody in the room. There was going to be some long, hard days. They would be exhausted and wish they could quit. At any time, the desire to make the climb would be traded for the desire to die or stop climbing. I told them, "If you ever get to a point where you begin to feel this way, speak up. Don't let people think you're okay and you're slowly drifting away from the support of the group".

I continued, "On top of that, if I become an eater of my own words and begin to fail you all, I need the group to hold me accountable. If I begin to break, snap me out of it. I need you to hold me up. I need you to keep me committed. We are a unit with a unified goal to reach the top of Mt. Altitude. Once we complete the goals, our names will be etched in history. Now, look. We will all have our names etched no matter what. But I ask you, what do you want to be remembered for? THIS… is the opportunity to leave behind something greater than you and I. This is the time to leave your mark and earn your spot. This is our day to leave a lasting impression on generations to come."

"With that said," I concluded. "if you start, I expect you to finish this. This game will not have a retry or pause button for your leisure. You either look this challenge square in the eye with me or you don't climb, period. God has pre-destined my ability to get this done. I am here today in order to fulfill the promises given to me. I have accepted my purpose to reach the top. We leave in the morning at 7am. Have your equipment ready to go, mindset in check, and be ready to give everything you have to achieve the purpose set for you. If your fear triumphs your will to fulfill your God-given destiny then, damnit, stay home and don't bother to show up. A man who can't assassinate his fears is a man willing to assassinate your dreams with the fears he retains. I pray to see you all in the morning."

When it was time to step off at 7am, 20 turned into 5 people. With the 6 of us left, I've never felt so at peace about our ability to get the climb done. I knew that with preparation, trust, and focus, we were ready.

## Preparation is the Father of Results

To be prepared is to condition your instincts. The more you prepare for your goals, the more the shark in you begins to smell blood in the water. When sharks smell blood in the water, they know that their prey is weak and their senses say, "Go get em!" When you do the proper preparation, your dreams look even more achievable and you're ready to attack them head on. Thinking through the process before the situation occurs can calm emotions when the feeling of "I've been here before, so let me act like it" sets in. Check out these three questions:

1. What if you studied and the teacher hits you with a pop quiz?
2. What if you are CPR trained and someone passes out in front of you?
3. What if you're competing for a championship and you've studied your opponent?

In each instance, do all of your fear and doubts go away? Not all of it, necessarily. But the amount of fear and doubt does decrease, right? The point I'm getting at is preparation is clearly tied to your emotions. You will never know if you've mastered a situation until it happens to you in real time and you're forced to react. If you've made the right preparation, when that situation arises, success will greet you on the other side. Real time situations will also inform you if you didn't prepare enough and dismiss you in the most brutal ways and have you going back to the drawing board.

I have always had the ambition to lead a team. The accolades never mattered to me, nor did the attaboys. I wanted the energy of winning and watching my team take their rightful place in greatness as I sat in the shadows. The minute my subconscious mind decided it wanted so little, every amount of negative energy in the world congregated to test me and prove that I wasn't worthy. The first test I received was when I was a young private in the Army.

When I was in basic training, I served as a student platoon sergeant responsible for leading close to 30 soldiers. The job was fairly challenging as a new leader thrown in the fire. I was responsible for effectively communicating information through my fellow leaders, getting everyone to training, as well as their medical appointments and maintaining accountability of their locations. When I look back now, it wasn't that difficult of a job but in the moment, it was just Hell On Wheels.

There was a female soldier in my platoon who didn't like me and was intentionally spiteful to me. She was cheeky and rude because I was selected over her as the student platoon sergeant. In retaliation and jealousy, she would intentionally show up late to formations claiming I didn't notify her of where she needed to be. She claimed I didn't send people to get her so she could be at the right place at the right time. She even claimed that I had it out for her, with the intent of destroying her reputation.

I eventually got tired of her always being late and her unwillingness to take responsibility for her actions. In basic training, if one messed up, we ALL messed up. We would all take punishment for one person's actions. But no matter who messed up, my fellow soldiers were only upset with one guy: me, the leader. I was the leader who was expected to hold everyone together and I didn't. The more and more soldiers around me started to get upset with me, the more alone and frustrated I felt.

I was young and trying to lead as a friend rather than as a leader. Not to mention, I had low self-esteem and I didn't realize my self-doubt affected my ability to lead and influence others. So every time this woman would be spiteful, it got to me. When all 30 of us paid for her actions, everyone took it out on me and that got to me as well. The fact that I was away from my family and friends, feeling out of place, it got to me. It got to me so much, I couldn't take it anymore.

I went to the Drill Sergeant's office with a head full of depression, but accepting that I couldn't do this anymore. I stood at the desk and told her, I couldn't do this anymore and that I'd like to resign my position. She looked at me in complete shock. She reminded me of my potential and where my career was going in the Army if I just held on and chose not to give up. She even disclosed that she knew the female soldier was out to break me. My drill sergeant caught her a few times walking into the women's barracks after I gave clear instructions.

She asked me if I was willing to get back out there again and give it another try. Even after telling me everything, my mind was at the brink of snapping and going off on everyone. I wanted to physically put my hands on people even though I knew that wasn't the mark of a leader. I decided the best thing for me to do was to relinquish my duties. I reaffirmed to the drill sergeant that I was done and that I'd like to resign. She granted my request.

It was an awkward moment because after she approved my resignation, her demeanor changed. I felt like a boy disappointing his mother. I saw the life drained out of her eyes. I felt neutral and calm as I walked out of her office. When I returned to the barracks, the rest of the platoon was coming from the dining hall after eating. We had earned the privilege to run back individually to the barracks without needing the entire platoon together.

Evidently, the word traveled that I quit had made it back to the barracks before I did. As soon as I passed the dining hall door, guess who came out the door? The female soldier who wanted me to quit so bad. And with confidence and pride in her heart, she pointed at me, smiled and said "Ha, I made you quit nigger." I had no response for her as she ran to the formation. I was in complete shock that she would even say that, which of course put all of the pieces together for me that she didn't like black people in positions of authority.

I was truly taken back and felt hollow. I felt terrible for quitting. Everything started to come to me. I had a chance to lead, and I quit. I didn't quit because my body wouldn't allow me to continue, or due to inappropriate conduct, but because of another person. I realized that I wanted to lead so bad and got the chance, but I never took the time to prepare myself for what would come with my responsibilities.

**Prepare the Mind**

Whatever consumes your mind controls your life. I believe if you could see the thoughts inside the minds of people who work intensively, you would understand their logic. I think you would see a section of the brain screaming out, "let's goooo!!!! Lets get this done! One more set of 10, one more lap around the track, on more paper!!!" You know what you would also find? You'd find the thoughts that say, "this sucks!!! Why are you doing this? This is heavy! Can you just stop?"

I say all of this from a standpoint of joking, but it's also true. Every mind is a battlefield with artillery firing on one side and tanks on the other. Before you enter into any mental war, you have to be ready.

**You're Not Hasn't Gotten It Done**

If you haven't achieved your goals and ambitions yet, that's because something hasn't shifted your desired outcome to the forefront. The system you're working right now isn't getting you there. If you look at what you're doing right now to achieve your goals, do you think that it's enough to get you where you want to be yet? Have you become a student of the craft you want to enter?

If you haven't done any of these, I'm going to be very honest with you. I expect you to achieve late or never. That means I expect you to achieve your goals later in life, which sadly by that time your vision could've already been realized by someone else. Or you could just never achieve it because you were unwilling to change your mindset Now, could it be that the universe doesn't want you to win? Or could it be that you are electing to continue the same cycle everyday with minimal contributions to your goals and expecting a high yield of results? If you put a few dollars in the stock market, don't expect large returns.

The most powerful tool you were gifted with was your mind because of the power it possesses. On the same token, the most dangerous tool you were gifted with was your mind because of the power it possesses. The mind is the physical contributor that archives your daily thoughts, ideas, records, and feelings. The mind designed the building you work in, cultivated the beans to enjoy your local coffee, and produced the educational tools to teach us all. However, before any of these were invented, a mind envisioned them and sent a signal through the body that human hands used to build them.

## They're Not Investing In The Company; They're Investing In You

The company you keep is crucial to solidifying your mark on the world. There are a chosen few who achieve their goals when they have others in their corner from day one. Normally, your team, image, and moves change as you progress.

Even the Bible makes it clear that we must be weary of the people we keep around us during our growing processes. If you keep the same people around you year after year and you see no genuine growth, then your circle needs to change.

---

*The company you keep should be worth more than just a hug and a smile.*

---

Now, this isn't to degrade the importance of having those types of people (hugging and smiling friends) in your life because we should all strive to bring happiness to those around us. In fact, this doesn't necessarily mean the people you have around you are bad people. But what it could mean is that you haven't found, or put yourself in a position to find, the people that you really need to grow.

So pump the brakes. I'm not telling you to abandon your friend that you grew up or partied with. I'm telling you to look at other relationships you can add to sharpen your skills, increase your focus, and build a better you. I'll tell you this, "hate" is such a terrible word, so I'll use "dislike" instead. I've always disliked when an opportunity is being offered and people tell me they are going to go and consult with someone who has NEVER DONE WHAT THEY WANT TO DO!

- Why are you consulting with a broke person on how to become rich?
- Why are you consulting with your friend in debt about how to best invest your money?
- Why are you asking for love advice from the guy who you know cheats on his wife?

All of these questions and concepts remind of a quote from the book, *The Richest Man in Babylon*:

> *"Advice is one thing that is freely given away, but watch that you take only what is worth having".*

Although, he's talking more about a man's savings, this can be applied to all avenues of your life. Define your company and what they must bring to the table in order to validate their worth and facilitate your success.

Growing up, my grandmother always told me, "Kenny, be careful of the company you keep. Not everybody is your friend. Some people are just your associates." To this day, I take that logic with me everywhere I go. It's unwise to accept that everybody in your corner is for you or will always be for you.

In fact, there are some people who didn't even have your best interest in mind from the beginning of your relationship. They can see potential in you and are willing to ride your wave until you make it where you are meant to go. Once you've achieved your greatness, they want their share of the pie they believe they "contributed" to. And if they don't get their fair share, then you're the traitor and not them. Even more sad, these people will have stayed in your presence so long that the thought process that you owe them could be in their subconscious. So what was originally a "scheme" that they were masterfully executing could be their own true reality as you and that person go through life experiences together. Be very careful in these types of situations.

---

*"Your with your fam, but your fam may not be with you." – Jidenna (A Bull's Tale)*

---

# DOPE Exercise 2: Draw the Line...Where Do You Stand in My Life?

When you want ice, you'll freeze water. When you want water, you'll melt ice. When you want exponential self-growth, you'll invest more time in yourself. When you want wise advisors around you, you'll adjust your inner circle. Jim Rohn has said best: "You cannot change your destination overnight, but you can change your direction overnight."

The people in your corner can only do one of four things to your life and we will discuss each person in much greater detail:

1. The "I'm Just Here" person: Not really your friend, but associates with you. (Associate)
2. The "As Long As You're Great, I'm Here" person: Your friend as long you provide benefits to them. As soon as you collapse or are at your worst, they are gone. (Gold-Digger/Deceiver)
3. The "What You Need, I Got Yo' Back" person: The friend that no matter what your next move is, they will lace up their boots and go to war with you. Even if it means dragging you through the fire, he/she will bring you out alive. (The Ride or Die)
4. The "I Know How to Get There, So I'll Teach

You" person: The one who knows how to get you to the next level and is willing to coach and teach you as long as you are willing to put in the work. (Gem Dropper/The Mentor)

Get a sheet of paper and write out the names of the people who are closest to you. Decide which of the four types of people those in your circle fall under. Do you have a heavy concentration of one or the other? Do you see the need to add a certain type of person or remove a certain type of person? Take a holistic look at your circle and decide if this circle is conducive to achieving your purpose in life.

# Chapter Three: Climate Change

The sound of the frozen winds screamed like sirens in search of their next victim. As we continued our climb up Mt. Altitude, the challenge became more daunting as we felt life's fatigue grasp strong hold on us. The cold air kissed our lips with an icy chill that could be felt through our bones and souls. The air became thinner with every step. The snow became deeper as we progressed towards the top. It was clear that this wasn't going to be an easy feat. With every change we physically felt, it felt much more painful in the confines of our minds. But as our environment changed, so did we. Some of us... not for the greater good.

I took lead walking in front of the group with over 18,000 feet to go. As we continued our climb, Lex approached me, walking by my side and said with a friendly tone, "Ken, can we ...you know... Take a break? We've been walking for a while now. We have to be at least 2,000 or 3,000 feet up by now. I can't be the only one who's tired. Is anyone else tired too?"

After Lex made his comment, the team yelled out almost in unison, "YEAH!"

I remained silent and continue to walk.

"We can take a small break, Ken. I promise everything will be okay. Let's just rest for a few. Then we can get right back on it."

I still continued to be quiet and walked. By this point in time, Lex's frustration continued to rise.

He turned back to me and said with authority, "You hear that?! Everyone is tired. And you're probably tired too and trying to act like a freaking superhero right now!"

I swallowed hard, pulled out my canteen, took a sip of water, and remained silent as I continued to trudge.

"Hello?! Ken?! Kennn!!! Oh I know, how about this? Since Ken can't hear, everyone in favor of taking a break right now, say I?!" Everyone raised their hands and said "I". At least, I assume everyone did… because I never turned around to count.

"Ken, do you see all of these hands saying, oh, I don't wanna die of fatigue or hypothermia on a FREAKING mountain away from my family and friends. Look back and see everyone with their hands up high!!!" I continued to look straight ahead, but my mentality began to change. The more I heard Lex's complaints, the more they began to become embedded into my mind.

I began to feel weaker, more tired, and frustrated. My confidence began to decline with every "STOP! WAIT! LET'S TAKE A BREAK!" The thoughts began to circle around in my head like vultures hovering over prey. It was like vultures were waiting to ensure I was dead so they could feed on my flesh. You see, I've never been the "give up so easily guy". Not since that situation in basic training. I vowed to never be that guy again. Now, I set my mind to a vision and I follow through. But to continue hearing the gripes and complaints of the people who chose to take this hike knowing the challenges and consequences for being weak were fatal were just too much for me. My heart began to beat faster. My eyes began to widen. I stomped harder into the snow. I began to breathe deeper… and deeper… and deeper… until I… just lost it.

"Kennn!!!", Lex said.

I shouted, "Enouuuuggghhhh!" I froze in my tracks and turned around to the group.

"Look, if you're tired of walking, go back down the freaking mountain. You knew this wasn't going to be easy. You also knew that this was going to require heart. And if this is what you call "heart", do me a favor and go into cardiac arrest right now!!! We are continuing to walk because we haven't reached a distance far enough to take a break. You break too long, and you won't even be able to make it to the next crest. You will die before we get there. Now is not the time to rest. It's time to dig deep and move. Once you get to the next crest, then you can take a break. But this isn't the time. As soon as your legs get tired, you want to rest. You don't get to where you want to be in life by constantly taking breaks as you get close to your next breakthrough. Reach a breakthrough FIRST and then you rest. Now, I don't want to hear another complaint today. Shut your mouth, focus on the goal, and let's get where we CAN rest. If you don't like it, too bad. Leave and good luck going back down. I'm going to the top. Roll with me or roll down the mountain, period. Now, there. I gave you your break. You're welcome."

I resumed walking. As I looked back around, everyone was silent as they continued to trudge. Some were looking at me as if I were crazy. But most importantly, everyone was still with me.

**The Company You Keep**

Remember when I said, the company you keep is crucial to solidifying your mark on the world? There are a chosen few who achieve their goals with people who have been there from the beginning. To be called a "Day One" friend is a special badge of honor to wear for two reasons.

1. Because you share that title with your Day One.
2. Because you can be more confident than the average person that your Day One has your back forsaking all others.

Normally, your team, image, and moves change as you evolve as a person. And sadly in your evolution, people change too. The girl that painted your nails and made you feel better when you were twelve may not be the one you call at twenty-five when you are overwhelmed with life's sorrows. Somewhere down the line, there will be a change in your starting five. You've got to be ready for that change in your team.

It's hard to believe at times that your team from the beginning may not be the team you finish with. But the truth is that people grow through seasons. In fact, you may have a friend that you're no longer as close with because they have outgrown you and you just haven't received the message yet. Ouch! I know it stings because I've been there. But it is what it is. Sadly, people outgrow each other.

> *"But it hurts more to find out someone has outgrown you than delivering the news you've outgrown them."*

Sometimes, you outgrow them and they realize it, so they let you go so you can become who you're destined to be. Why would they let you go? Because real friends are okay with watching you from afar if they know being close will hold you back.

But as far as people in your life go, adapting to your environment will involve building a powerful team around you. Now powerful doesn't mean they have to be able to buy everything or be masterminds at building schemes. This just means they are strong enough in thought and influence to encourage you to grow and to build you into the person that you were destined to be. They'll even block the people out of your life that are there to destroy you when you are too ignorant or in your feelings to see it for yourself.

**Friends over Love**

Back in the early 2000s, I was dating a girl named Nikki. And yes, she is a real person and not a Prince reference. If you didn't get that joke, go talk to some folks that are 30 years old and beyond. Anyway, I was crazy over this girl. She was smart, funny, and in my opinion had the most banging body I had ever seen in my life. Now, I'm not sexist or anything, but I know that when I pick a woman to be with, I'm a man of exquisite taste. See, there's another Prince reference right over your head.

So Nikki and I continued to get more serious as time progressed. And the more serious she and I became, the less I began to care about doing things like music, business, art, and networking. All I wanted to do was stay home and chill with her. Now with any person you're with, there's compromise involved. You may not be able to connect with everybody perfectly. And believe me, she was no different. Nikki was a drinker, smoker, twerker, and all of that. In short, she was a college girl who was out to just have a good time.

Now, me…. I was the complete opposite. I was an Army guy looking to become an officer. I was a scholar, track runner, class president, and had everything I needed in the palm of my hand to take my life to the next level. I only had one weakness in my world: a pretty woman who could hold a brother down. And make no mistake about it, she did all that and more.

Now my routine used to be early morning wake ups, workouts, class, meetings, studying, and goal writing. After I met her, it turned into, early morning alarm hitting, late to Army workouts which meant an automatic butt chewing, sitting in class tired from drinking the night prior, and getting off work to drink and chill with her. Needless to say, the way I lived changed and clearly it wasn't for the better based on the potential I possessed.

One day, a good friend of mine named Will approached me. He sat me down with the most stern, deep voice, looked me in my eyes and said, "YO look! This girl is killing you, son. You don't dress the same, talk the same, you don't show up to events anymore. And you're the class president. This ain't what real men do. I think it's that girl, bruh."

## Altitude

As soon as I got ready to explain to him how she upgraded me as a person, he cut me off and said, "And you better not talk about she upgraded you. Ain't nobody start talking about upgrading nobody until Beyonce's album came out. So let's put that foolishness to the side. This girl is on that Fuggees-ish; killing you softly. You are one of the few guys here that everybody knows is going somewhere. And you out in these streets with a chick that don't even love you like that and letting her crush your image as a man. How long until she has you smoking and you fail a piss test? Before you know it, you'll be out here trying to find a job because you didn't do the right thing. If she isn't elevating you, you need to start elevating her. And if she ain't for the elevating, get her off the elevator!"

That last line stuck with me the rest of my life. If people don't want to elevate with you, get 'em off the elevator.

---

*You ever noticed that no one wants to get on the elevator with someone going in the opposite direction?*

---

It's because you don't want to hold the other person back. Well I have got news for you, you're on an elevator on the way and when the doors open for someone to enter your elevator, before they walk though the door, be sure to ask them, "Going up?" Because if they say they're going down, don't let them on!! Sorry, this elevator is full. Even if you're elevator fits 12 people and you're the only one on it! NO, YOUR ELEVATOR IS FULL. Don't be ashamed to put it out there.

I'll tell you this too: some people are great at concealing their intentions. They will make themselves appear as if they are ready to support your initiatives. The truth is, they see potential in you that no one else sees and they want to get to you so they can ride your wave. It's like a stock in the market that you see clearly is going to make you some money. So what do you do? You buy it and you get as much as you can. But the other side of that example is that once it doesn't make the money that it once made, it becomes an option rather than a priority. Keep your eyes open and be prepared to adapt when it comes to people.

**Bodak Yellow**

Bodak Yellow was one of the hottest songs in 2017 and 2018 and to keep it real with you, it's still fire now. When that song first came on, one line in the whole track really caught my attention:

---

*"I don't dance now, I make money moves. Said I don't gotta dance, I make money moves." – Cardi B*

---

With those two bars, Cardi B summed up the last decade of her life. She was a former stripper turned hottest female rapper out at the time. Now that she placed herself in a position to start making deals, build a network, and make money, she wasted no time to go through the evolution from stripper to boss. Now, anyone who keeps up with Cardi B on Instagram knows she's still the same ol' Cardi. Cool, ratchet, and hilarious.

If the way you move today is the same way you moved a decade from now, trust me when I say YOU'VE WASTED A DECADE. There are constantly changes going on in society from technological advances, international events, and more. As situations happen, there has to be a shift in the moves of the people around you. What do you call a person who stands still while everything else is moving? An easy target.

---

*When you choose to sit still, you open the doors of the obsolete.*

---

You know what always frustrated me while I was young? I had buddies that I would go to the park with. And after a quick game of basketball, we would lie on the ground and stare up at the sky. And while looking at the sky, we would talk about our dreams and ambitions. But while talking, one guy would always go from speaking about his dreams or speaking them into existence, and he would just start ranting.

"Why can't I be that dude?" or "I sure wish I was rich like that. I'd be out here balling with my money until it's all gone." he'd say.

The only thing I'd think to myself was, "and that's why you don't have it. You haven't evolved in thought well enough to command the things that you desire to come to you." I'm a firm believer that faith without works is dead. So if you don't put in work, expect your dreams to remain dead. So some of you right now are like, "Alright, Ken, I got it. You keep talking about evolving and adapting. How do you know when it's time to evolve or better yet, how do I evolve?" Don't worry... I've got the answers for you. When any of the following occur, it's time.

**You're Comfortable**

Congratulations, you finally adapted to your current climate and everyday life has become easy. You don't have to work hard anymore because you know all of the answers. Everything is going your way and you don't have to do anymore to grow…. If any of these statements have been you recently, you are too comfortable.

While you are getting comfortable, someone is stepping out of his or her comfort zone. Complacency starts peeking at you to see if you're open to it paying you a visit. The names that are remembered are the ones who improved their lane in the way that would change their field or industry forever. I want you uncomfortable because that's where new challenges approach.

"But why do you want me uncomfortable? Don't you want me to be the best in the room?" Absolutely I do! But here's the realist comment so far in the book:

*"If you're the smartest guy or gal in the room, you're in trouble. Being the smartest can prevent bright minds from becoming smarter."*

Leaders don't sit in the room with all the knowledge and wisdom just to tell a room full of subordinates and peers how they want something done. They recruit the best and brightest in their respective fields. That way, when the leader doesn't know the answer, someone on the team does.

To keep it very honest with you, someone reading this book feels like they're the best because they are fearful of what the next challenge holds. Which brings me to the next reason why it's time for a change.

**You Need a Challenge**

Human beings are built to survive adversity and to celebrate conquering fears and doubts. When the job looks huge, that's when we get hype! We start wanting to step our game up. At least, that's what I've seen. But then again I surround myself with those who want to take that next step up. What if I told you the promotion you're looking for will require you to stay up late nights studying the company, learn a field you know nothing about, and may require a significant amount of overtime for the first couple of months . . . BUT, there's also a $30,000 pay jump per year? Would you be okay with that? Some would say yes. Some would say no. But what's always entertaining to find out is the reason behind why they won't take the job. Some won't take the job because they don't want the late hours. They don't want the hard work. They don't want to put in the extra time away from the office to get smarter at their craft. However, the same people unwilling to work harder would like to stay in the same job and ask for a raise.

Look, even video games get boring if you play the same level over and over again. If you want to get your money up, boss up. If you want to really lead, take the opportunities that require more effort. Don't look for the easy way out. It's better to adapt in a growing environment than to be complacent in a stagnant environment. Take the challenge of adapting in a new environment. In four words: To grow, seek discomfort.

**Monotony**

Life isn't built to be the same every single day. When everything starts to blend together, it's definitely time for a change. Boredom welcomes complacency and you have that in your life. You can't continue to live in boredom and expect excitement. It may be time to switch the game up so that you become better. It may even be time to adventure out and try something new.

I started to become fed up with life as a senior military Captain. I joined the Army with the expectation of having a riveting life where I would spend my days in the field or deployed. I had visions of planning major Army operations, kicking down doors, and being in combat during major firefights. In actuality, I was editing slide decks and watching people kick in doors and do all the work that I wanted to do. I realized how much I hated being a desk jockey. I wanted to get from behind the desk and into the game.

In those moments of irritation, I started to search for what I wanted to do next with my life. Then one day, I was blessed with an assignment that changed my course. I was assigned to escort Heisman Winner and retired Brigadeer General Pete Dawkins during the 2018 Army All American Bowl. That was an experience unlike any other I had ever witnessed in my life. While escorting him, I was offered an opportunity to shadow him as he gave inspirational speeches to future NFL superstars, consulting with media broadcasters, and so much more.

But what mattered most to me was the man himself and how he led his life. He was a kind gentlemen who was very quick to tell you he had moments behind the desk but preferred to be out and about at events doing great things. He was also very kind when speaking with his wife and daughter. In fact, he spoke to his daughter like she was still in her teens. The last thing that caught my attention was how Mr. Dawkins walked out in front of a packed arena and received such loud cheers and praise from the fans in the stands and yet he remained humble and proud to be present.

The last moment I had with Mr. Dawkins was dropping him off at the airport the day after the game. He looked at me and said, "Ken, whether you decide to stay in the military or leave, no matter what you do next, I know you will be successful." That compliment meant the world to me because a football and military legend reaffirmed to me that I possessed the potential to go to the next height in Altitude. In that moment, I realized that this was how I wanted to lead my life. I wanted that feeling forever. I wanted the nostalgia that comes with being in a room of cheering fans inspired by what's center stage. Mr. Dawkins at the All American Bowl set the stage for me to build a brand that would be bigger than me. But I knew in order to taste that energy again, it couldn't be done while in the military; or could it?

**Life is a Test**

Life is one big evaluation. The instructor is the universe, and the instructor doesn't care about whether you pass or fail. When a test is given, the level of difficulty for each question varies. But at the end of the day, your evaluator (life) doesn't care about question difficulty. Life cares about how many you got right or wrong.

Therefore, you have to treat your life accordingly. You will go through a lot of positive moments. You'll also see some minor roadblocks that you can resolve with minimal action. And let's not ignore the fact that eventually, you will go through situations that will test the man or woman in your soul and not just your mind. Empathy doesn't pause your evaluation. On top of that, apathy doesn't overwrite judgment. Our society is based on judgment from others and based on what you do daily, that has no bearing on them..

Therefore as new challenges arise in your life, you've got to continue to adapt to each scenario presented. To check to see if you're truly growing daily, I challenge you to answer this one question daily: "Do I deserve to be here?" If you ever have to question if you made the right choice, it's time to seek out wise counsel. But to go further, the answer to the question may seem simple but people get it wrong every single day. Life is so much more than getting up out of bed, doing your daily routine, and going back to sleep.

**React to Contact**

In the military there is a tactical drill called "React to Contact" where we engage situations as they appear. That doesn't mean you aren't prepared for the situation when it appears, it means you accept that the situation is imminent and you need to be ready to react. It's a fact of life that situations are going to happen that we aren't always prepared for. I wasn't prepared for my grandfather to pass away while I was still in my 20s. I wasn't prepared to sign on the dotted line for my daughter to have open-heart surgery at seven days old. To be honest, I wasn't ready for the alarm clock to go off 30 minutes late this morning to put me behind the power curve. But as situations occur, we have an opportunity to view our position and determine how we can prepare ourselves for them before they fully unfold. What has always worked well for me was making time to write out my weekly plan over the weekend. Here's how I lay out my week to balance my schedule

## Ken's Libra Scale Technique (How I Balance My Schedule):

- Layout every mandatory event for the week from work (secure the money, first!).
- Review personal events to place on the calendar (appointments, bills due).
- Add in habits that require calendar space (workouts, sleep hours, family time, etc.).
- Review my bank account (the bank account will always tell you what you can and can't do).
- Start reviewing this week's calendar by looking three weeks out (something week's out may have a pre-requisite that needs to be completed this week).

# DOPE Exercise 3: Balancing the Libra Scale

Let's balance the Libra Scale together. You've seen how I lay out my schedule. Now, I want you to lay out yours. Get a sheet of paper and write out how you are currently balancing your schedule. In addition, how could you better manage your time?

# Chapter Four:
## Take the Road Less Traveled

As nightfall hit, we reached our rest point.

"Phew! I am tired", said Lex. Everyone began slapping high-fives and cheering, including me.

"Alright guys, everyone come on over here," I said. The team gathered around me. "Listen up, we've done well. Now let's set up camp for the night. Make sure the stakes are buried deep in the ground. You don't want your tent to fly away, right? Especially with you in it." Everyone laughed at my poor attempt at a joke.

I continued, "I'll start a fire up. As soon as you set up camp, get warm and get rest. Is everyone on the same page?" Everyone nodded their heads and disbanded to start working on their areas.

After creating the fire, I shouted, "Lex! Come with me." Lex immediately broke away from his work and ran over to me with a big smile, breathing heavy.

Panting, he said, "What's up, Ken?"

"Lex, we're heading up again tomorrow morning." I laid out a map in front of the fire. Here's how we're going to get there." I explained our plan for tomorrow's hike.

"This is a joke, right?! You really want to climb straight up? Do you know how dangerous it'll be going that way?" Lex asked.

"What's the matter? You make it sound to me like you can't climb or something. Listen, we make this climb, it saves us time, and we rest longer overnight before we continue hiking again."

"I don't know Ken. I feel like this is really risky. We are going to put ourselves in a lot of danger doing this," Lex warned.

"Listen, it's going to keep snowing. If we continue to walk straight around this mountain, we are eventually going to meet snow too soft and deep to continue moving through. We are doing this, Lex. Sometimes, to get where you want to go in life, you have to take the road less traveled."

Lex nodded his head. "Fine, Ken. We've already started this climb. We can't stop here now. I'll let the team know." Lex walked away and told the team. Everyone set their tents, reset their gear, and started getting ready for the next day's climb.

## The Power of the Process

The easy road for a man to walk is the road that leads to accepting his failure, faults, and place in life as second-class. But the man who is willing to take the extra steps to have his name in lights is who is known forever. Taking the road less traveled produces immortals. It produces people "statued" in time rather than frozen in it. In life, many options will be presented to you to avert from your path and take the easy way out. The minds of you and those closest to you will be tested. But in the midst of that storm, what are you going to do? Will you cower and take the easy way out or rise to the occasion and walk the road of certain danger knowing you will survive?

I don't like pressure; I love it now. As a young man, I placed pressure on myself to become the greatest version of Ken humanly possible. So I laid out everything that I wanted to complete and committed to making it a reality. Let me say to you,

> *...the moment you declare that you want to be or do something; you have personally granted the universe an opportunity to test your soul for confirmation.*

It will start presenting challenges that you never expected. What was once so easy becomes a little more challenging.

The early morning wake up calls start to get a little more difficult. That snooze button starts to look very attractive. If you're a smoker trying to quit, does the pack of cigarettes behind the counter look more attractive just because the company changed their package? Those honey buns you like went on sale from $1.20 to .50. Your spouse or significant other becomes moody because you are focused on building a business plan or writing a play and not spending as much time with them. You're ready to give up a lifestyle that wasn't helping you win and now your friends are saying you've changed.

**The Heat of Ambition**

But how ironic is it that this doesn't happen until you want to step your game up? It seems like you said what you wanted and all of a sudden, BOOM! The world is against you and ready to defeat you at every turn. You can't run, quit, submit, or anything. I call that immediate pressure you feel the Heat of Ambition. See Proverbs 18:21 states, *"Death and life are in the tongue"*. Therefore, when you speak life, death will always exercise its right to rebut your claims. The Heat of Ambition is defined as any form of opposition that arises AFTER YOU SELF-PROPHECY with the purpose of validating your claims. This is why I like to tell people who always say "claim it in advance" to ensure they are ready for the challenge in advance too. Keep that same energy for both. If you start feeling any of the following signs or symptoms, there's a high chance that you are feeling the Heat of Ambition right now.

**More Haters**

Wooh! I'd like to start this point off with a disclaimer. I never like discussing haters because that gives them energy and relevancy. They are recognized long enough for me to thank them for adding fuel to my fire as we continue to grow. Now back on topic, if you begin a new venture, project, or lifestyle change and it produces more negative press about you, believe me when I say that you are winning in some facet. In the *48 Laws of Power* by Robert Greene, Law #6 states that you should *"Court Attention at All Costs"*. Haters will take your positive moves and attempt to make them into negative press. In those moments, this will turn into one of your forks in the road. You could always engage the haters directly or go on a public relations (PR) spree to let people know you are not who they are portraying you to be. But, the way I like to handle this is to let them talk. There's a song by a singer named Jidenna called "Some Kind of Way". The chorus of the song says it's all:

> *"No matter what you say or where you go, or what you do, or how you pray, somebody's gonna feel some kind of way about you". - Jidenna*

This could not be a truer statement. There will always be bad press for you just like there is great press. I mean, if they were willing to crucify Jesus, you are merely a man. Some people tend to forget that, but you should never forget it. If you see an increase in haters, don't fret. You're doing the right thing. This is a clear sign to do two things: reflect on what you're doing to ensure it's moral and ethically sound, and decide if there's anything you need to address immediately that could actually hurt you long-term. If neither of these reflective statements render any uncomforting responses, then forget about the haters, wink at them, and continue to *#bossup.*

**Friends Turn Into Enemies**

There's nothing more disappointing than a friend becoming an enemy. But when you decide to become the best version of you, it may not only require you to cease doing things you used to do; it could also eliminate friends and loved ones by default. You may be ready for the next height in altitude but they aren't. When you decide to grow and your friend is not ready to rise with you, a change will happen. They won't even take the time to realize that they've elected to stay the same. When those moments happen, you just have to accept that this is merely another sign that the road you've elected to take is about to reap great rewards. You've probably got something that they want or you did something they couldn't do. Once you declared the road you want to take, they assumed you think you are better than them. Don't be blind. These people exist and sometimes they are right in front of you. Love with a big heart, but move with little baggage.

**More Failure:**

If you take nothing else from this chapter, read and internalize these next lines. Even when you are performing at the highest heights, people will still tell you no. It's not that you're terrible. It's not that you haven't put in the work. It's not that you haven't taken the correct road on the pathway to your dreams; it's just that the road can sometimes come with curves. One of our greatest gifts as human beings is the ability to visualize. We create things in our mind that have never existed on this earth. We can think and visualize our next 24 hours, envision how our child's birthday party is going to go, and even feel reactions in the present for future events. But know that just because your vision is great doesn't mean that every man will see your vision. That's the reason your vision was given to you. If everyone said yes to your dream, would your dream feel that special to you? I doubt it. We need adversity. We need challenges to stretch us and mold us into the best "us" possible.

---

*There is no growth without "OW".*

---

If someone turns you down, then they helped guide you onto the path to your achievements, be thankful they did. If you fail at something, be okay with the fact that you failed. Failure isn't a step backwards. It's just crossing wrong answers off the list. The good news is if you don't let failure rule you, eventually the only answer left will be the right one. If your ideas are turned down, they may need some tweaking. The responses given to you during failure cold turn a $1M dollar project into a $1B company. Trying to find love could turn a bad divorce into meeting the love of your life. I know this better than anyone because that was me.

**Beasts Begin to Appear Bigger:**

There was a time when I wanted a degree just to say I had a degree. To be honest, I couldn't have cared less about it at that time. Now, luckily, the degree I obtained helped me later on in life when I started a business and other ventures that allowed me to help those around me. But there was a time when I questioned why I was even doing this right now? At the time, I felt like I was sitting up trying to get a degree I'd never use. I didn't want to sit at a desk all day. I wanted to be a choreographer who made dance routines for some of the best dancers in hip-hop. Dance was my love and my passion. But, as I grew older and served time in the military, I eventually got tired and my body began to deteriorate. Before I knew it, I was diagnosed with degenerative bone disease in my lower back and informed that it may be time to kiss dancing goodbye. When I reflect now, I have times where I wonder if the door on dancing was closed because I found my true calling or if I walked away from my true calling to do something else. That's a question I will never know the answer to and my major reason for imploring you to do what you love and walk that path no matter how difficult or impossible it may look. You could walk past destiny. And let me tell you, destiny won't give you a second thought if you do.

When I originally went to school, I went to get a bachelor's degree in chemistry. I was a very smart guy and knew that I could handle the work that came along with being a scientist. When I got into the core classes of chemistry, I thought I wanted to become a research scientist. I didn't have anything in particular research field I wanted to get into, but I know I saw myself in a white coat walking around a lab, mixing up chemicals in a tube, and presenting my discoveries before national boards and councils. I was going to find the cure to Cancer, HIV, diabetes, or something great.

However, what I eventually found out was that although I was smart, I wasn't ready for the daunting challenge that came with chemistry. I wasn't ready to become a committed student to the game and learning all of the tricks. Not to mention, classes kept getting more difficult as the semesters passed. I eventually found myself in a class with a professor that gave out Cs and Ds for majority of the semester. Through extra credit I found myself home free getting away a B in his class, but what scared me was knowing that medical school would eventually get here. And if I can't understand basic chemistry, how am I going to understand how to do proper research and development? How do I prove to grad school professors that I'm worthy of becoming a PhD? In fear, I ran from Chemistry to Political Science. This is a situation that I genuinely regretted for a while. Pain creeps in at its worst, making challenges look larger than they truly are. In the heat of trying to realize your potential, small setbacks can appear as giant the closer you step to your end goal. You can only blame you for quitting and giving up. So I had to fix this some way, somehow.

When I realized that I ran from my fears in my senior year of college at Fayetteville State University, I committed to do something that would allow me a chance to redeem myself. When commissioning to become an Army Officer, I joined the Chemical Corps. This would put me around science the rest of my military career. After a decade of military service, I can confidently say, I've never felt so proud of my decision to not give up on my goal to be part of the science community.

The message I'm sending here is no matter what, you've got to close the deal. When the beast looks bigger, that is a scare tactic created by the opposition to make you fear the goal.

---

*The only way to defeat this beast is to prepare for it, destroy it and leave not even a speck of dust in your wake.*

---

Make the beasts that stand in your way regret the day they stood before you. They didn't know how locked in you were. They didn't know you had something to prove to you and only you. They didn't respect their opponent so you had to make them pay for it and you don't take accounts receivable. There is no one who can measure your potential like you can. You are David before Goliath and your dreams are the slingshot and rock. Sling the rock and slay the beast! There's only room for one giant in this room. In the words of Queen Mother Ramonda in the movie Black Panther, **"Show them who you are."**

**James and Anil**

Attempting to take the easy way will never yield the reward that taking the road less traveled will. On the most challenging roads, you learn lessons that will never be learned if you take the easy way out. On the easy road, there are shortcuts, less threats, answers given out freely, and participation trophies. If you want to earn your way to the top, it will take true work and that only comes from going all the way and being all in. Let me tell you a story to bring this all together.

There were once two college freshmen and friends named James and Anil. They both had ambitions of one day becoming professional football players. James is a kid who came from poor beginnings while Anil came from a family with two generations of athletes. James woke up daily feeling like he had something to prove, while Anil didn't put his heart into the game because he knew he would get into the NFL solely based on the merit of his family's name. Four years passed and they were both selected to the NFL. Anil went $1^{st}$ round and James went $3^{rd}$ round. However, as the years progress, Anil got exposed as a lackluster player, and was proven to not be worthy of a $1^{st}$ round draft pick. James, on the other hand, proved to be a steal from the draft and he was moved to the starting lineup. When James and Anil's careers ended, Anil inducted his friend James into the Hall of Fame. And sadly, Anil never went.

Anil never put his heart into the process so he never went all the way. The reason he didn't go all the way (Hall of Fame) is because he wasn't truly in from day one. You have to commit fully or you are destined to fail or fall short of the ultimate success. It's almost guaranteed. This isn't to say that if you have a family in a business, you'll slack off. But this does go to show you that if you slack off because you think you are entitled, eventually your hustle, drive, and work ethic will shine through. One way or another, those who are not truly committed will always be exposed. Eventually, you have to begin putting work. The minute you begin taking breaks and slacking off is when you begin to crumble. Lastly, notice that both men made it to the league; but only one made it into the Hall of Fame. The one who made it to the Hall of Fame is the man who was all in. So let me ask you: What type of performance are you putting on and is it hall of fame worthy? Time will tell…

**The Process is the Product**

Does any of this sound familiar? I wake up daily like,

> *"Bruh! Why am I doing this?! I wake up everyday and nothing changes. I shower, workout, eat, go to work, come home, eat, watch TV, and sleep. I know some people are fine with this, but that's just not me. I legit hate this. It's frustrating. This never changes. What*

*am I doing wrong? The only changes I get are negative after negative after another negative issue. I'm just tired! Like, this just isn't fun anymore. Having few to nothing to do is making me sick. I can't take this much longer. I'm only in this job because my family and I gotta eat. What happened to my dreams? I wanted to dance, sing, fly a plane, own a business, travel worldwide and a bunch of other stuff. Now I'm here. So much for my dreams and ambitions. My face is going to break if I keep on handing out fake smiles. I'm depressed and frustrated with myself. It just seems like the higher I climb the more frustrated I become. What's a man supposed to do? Sit around and act like everything is cool? Because it isn't. I wanted the next level so bad! Hell, I still do! Why not me? Why can't it be me? Why can't I be the man! Why can't I be the guy? I'm the best and I know they can't be me. It's not fair. It's not FAIR!"*

---

Look, the process is the product. The product you want is success. Everyone creates their own versions of success. Therefore, the process yields varied results for every person involved. If someone chooses to rob a bank and gets arrested, the product of the process is jail. Because of the energy you put in to going to jail, you got your wish. If you smoke cigarettes on a daily basis, the process is still the product. The product is a damaged body, browned teeth, lung cancer and an assortment of other issues. But if you condition your body, join the Army, and graduate from basic training, then you have successfully become a soldier. What I'm saying is that your actions are all part of the process. It's all part of a bigger picture. If you reflect on some of the major incidents that happened in your life, you'll find that you knew what was coming before it happened.

If you can't verbally say what your results are going to be, that is your indicator that you only have an idea, not a plan. This is the exact reason why it's important for you to map out your moves very carefully. You can't be complacent about your moves. **Complacency is the new curiosity: They both killed the cat.** No matter what, your process will conclude with a product. So ask yourself, "Based on the process I'm producing right now, IN THIS MOMENT, what is my product going to be?" Break down the process into as many mini-steps as you need to, but have a plan. You retain the right to control parts of the process. Control them when you can.

### The Promise That Pain Will Come

No matter how fast you ride and no matter how much camouflage you wear, pain is coming for you once you've stated your desired to become something greater. What you can't predict is the amount of pain you will have to endure before reaching the end of the road. The climb will never end with you arriving at the top with no damage. That type of climb just doesn't exist. In fact, if you find a road to success with no bumps at all, please contact me because I want to see it. Just kidding; after the process is the product, right? Right! Anyway, to get to the top of a mountain, there will be slips, trips, lack of air, bumps, bruises, and more. This example also imitates life. Here's an instance where pain came for me on my road to becoming the best me.

After months of being a Army commander, the frustration of being cursed out daily, told I was going to be fired weekly by the senior operations officer, and being made out to be someone I wasn't by my company leadership, I was beginning to break down. Mentally, I was distraught. I was placed in a position to believe that I couldn't go to my Battalion or Brigade Commander for help because they wouldn't be on my side, nonetheless hear me out. I didn't know what to do. Now granted, I'm not perfect. I had my days when I missed deadlines, lashed out when things didn't get done, and felt the pressure of having leaders who were leader in authority only.

But as months passed, the pressure began to build on me. It was clear that they were sending certain leaders to my company and my meetings in preparations to groom them to take my place. There's nothing like knowing that you are giving it all you have and those above you don't want you there so they begin to make preparations to replace you. Eventually, after an investigation was brought against me for being a poor leader, I found myself on leave and with my family preparing for my daughter's birth. While on leave, I found out that almost half of the people who were smiling in my face were the same people making sworn statements against me. On top of that, the legal aid who redacted my investigation documents did it incorrectly so I was able to see the names of every person who smiled in my face and stabbed me slowly through my back and twisted the knife.

To think, on top of coming to work feeling mentally abused on a daily basis combined with my daughter's approaching open hear surgery, I was removed from my dream job. But, it was positive getting away from everyone, the drama, the controversy, the backstabbing, and all of that. However, a new pain was developing in my heart. That pain eventually pulled me into a dark place that I didn't think I'd be able to climb out of. I went into the "What If" zone. This zone is something like in The Dark Knight Rises after Bane pummels Batman. He drops him off at a place called Hell on Earth which is located in the Middle East. Bruce spends forever working on his body and mental just to trying and climb out of Hell on Earth, but during every escape attempt, he would miss the cliffhanger and fall at least 10 feet and be snapped backwards by an unforgiving rope. He had to have nights where he thought to himself, "What if I can't get out of here? What if I'm stuck here forever? Why am I here right now? It's just not right."

There was a time when I saw myself in my late 30s and early 40s sitting around the table and driving the future operations that would occur in the military. But that thought process was changed and it became disappointment and embarrassment. I felt terrible sitting in rooms full of new people who didn't even know who I was. It hurt knowing no matter how well I spoke, performed, or any of that, I was done. That was painful. It was a dark spot to be in. I felt depressed and was on the verge on suicide everyday for almost four months. I had to drive by the mountains to go home and considered just driving off the cliff multiple times just so my kids and wife could pay off their debt and live in financial peace. What made it worse was when my daughter was born. I still belonged to the unit where the incident occurred. This made me suffer even more. Because when I needed to go see my child be born, I had to stay in communication with them.

You couldn't have told me in that moment that God had a bigger plan for my life. He handed me over to my enemies and let them treat me as they wished. It was hard for me. To make it even worse, my battle buddy (First Sergeant) was placed under investigation too for a separate issue. All of this turned into a very interesting situation because we were the only dually black command team in the unit. The constant random check ups, meetings catered just to us, and embarrassing moments made in front of the entire command were just wrong. I was disrespected in public on multiple occasions and after everything was said, the guy who tore me down would send me back to my unit expecting me to lead like he hadn't intentionally tried to crush my spirit. To end it all, I found out people were commenting on my desire to "blackerize" my unit.

Although it was a very sad situation, I see it as the greatest blessing to ever happen in my life. It shaped me into the guy I am today. It angered me but humbled me. It showed me that those who smile when you're their leader aren't necessarily there for you. They could be smiling because they want you to stroke the ink pin in their favor when the time comes. I realized that suicide is not the way. I found a new level of resilience and realized that I was stronger than my father, who took his own life. It taught me so many life lessons about people, and it made into the guy I am right now.

*Pain will come... but enduring
leads to victory.*

# DOPE Exercise 4: Define the Product to Develop the Process

For you to develop a process, you have to know the product. What is it that you genuinely want to accomplish? What is on your heart that, if it's complete, will take you to the next level of altitude? On a sheet of paper, I want you to write out what your product, or end goal, will look like at the end of your process. Now, when you write this, I want you to get as detailed as you can. I mean get meticulous. We are talking about the great <insert your name>. You are always detailed. You always have a clear vision. So go deep. Down to the name of the project/company, size of the buildings, how much money it's going to bring you, who it will allow you to meet, and more. Once you've written this out, you've affirmed what you want to do.

Next, I want to you to lay out everything in this moment right now, while the energy is ablaze and your thoughts are fresh after reading this content. On that same sheet of paper tell me what the process looks likes to achieve these goals. Does the process look like a change of dress? Are you putting down a drink? Are you taking her out on more dates? Are you getting a personal trainer? Is this the last time he will talk to you like that? This is your moment. Write what must change in order for you to get there. Don't forget to timestamp the date you wrote this. Once there is a date, there is a reflective point.

# Chapter Five:
# The Power of the Mind

After we packed up our gear, everyone prepared their climbing and rappel gear. As I turned and looked the team in their eyes, I saw a few things. I saw the fear of being in the sky and knowing one loose rock could plummet someone to his or her death. I saw the excitement of moving and getting closer to the top of the mountain. I even saw a look of anxiety yet redemption in the eyes of some of our teammates.

To cool the fears and anxiety, I decided to speak to the team.

"This is a moment of mind over matter. If you're afraid to climb versus walk, I've got news for you: It's okay to be afraid. Because so am I. Some of you are afraid of failing. That's okay too. I've failed more in my life than I have ever succeeded, but now is a time to take every single one of those losses and leverage them to win in this one moment. And I can't speak for anyone else, but I intend to win. So yes, ladies and gentlemen, I'm fearful as well. But right now is not the time to stop. Now is the time to focus. It's time to get locked in and excited to win. We have each other and that's all we need right now. Don't fret. Breathe and think positively. At the end of all this when you are in the comfort of your homes, these moments will be legendary to you. The time for talking about making it to the next level is over. It's time to climb. I'll take lead. Follow me."

Everyone nodded their heads in confirmation that they were ready. I turned around and stabbed the frozen mountain with my ice pick. From there, there were no more words. To quote Elvis, it was time for "A little less conversation, a little more action."

**Use Your Mind**

It's hard to deal with a loss, or even with a win, if you don't take time to soak it all up. It's important to just take time to yourself and to vibe alone. I like to tell my friends that the worst place to leave a man is in silence, but the truth is it's only dangerous for a man who hasn't taken time to learn how his mind works. So during this chapter, we're going to talk through the power of your mind and how much potential is in it.

Your mind is pivotal to you winning in every aspect of your life. The day you decide to stop using your mind for growth is the day you die. What if I told you that dead men were in your presence on a daily basis? Well, I just told you. We literally live with the walking dead. Daily, you are in the presence of men and women who have given up on their dreams, disregarded their purpose, submitted to their addictions, and saw more value in meritocracy than greatness. We see this all but the question that sticks out in many minds is always the same: Why?

Why did you just give up on the goal? Did you know how close you were? Could you see all the people who were counting on you? Did you think about the generation coming after you? The answer is... none of these questions are relevant to a soul that longer cares. The moment a man loses his purpose, he is guaranteed to perish.

When people have seen what they consider as the end of the road, they lose their drive. The end of the road means they can see no sign of hope, no room for a resilient comeback, and a chance at redemption. And to be brutally honest about it, the world around them doesn't make it any easier on them. They will find that as they rise, the crabs in the barrel will pull them back in. When they fall, the same people who pulled them down want to mourn their collapse, but only for a short time. Then they're back to trying to find the next big star that they can take down while the recent falling star is struggling to burn bright.

These people are everywhere around you. What's even scarier is that, as we have found throughout time, no man is exempt from being that falling star. But, on a positive note, no man or woman has to allow themselves to fall. And lastly, if you should fall from grace, you are never too down to rise. Let's talk about how to build the mindset that builds what in the poem "Invictus" is known as an unconquerable soul.

**Develop the Escalator Complex**

Now what I'm about to introduce to you is what I like to call EC. If you read the subtitle, you already know what EC stands for. You see, when my grandfather passed, a friend of his told me, "Life is like an elevator because it's full of its ups and downs, but the good news is, once you go down, you can always rise back up."

This phrase really inspired me and kept me focused during a hard period of time in my life.

I was an MBA student, with a full-time job as a military officer. I had three kids and a wife that was overwhelmed with balancing kids, school, and trying to get back into the work force. I had a grandmother who was grieving after losing her best friend and was trying to figure out how she was going to live the rest of her life as a widow. My son was experiencing speech challenges, and my confidence was shaken after having to relinquish command due to a shaky investigation. Although everything he said to me in that moment was great, I had a difficult time as a person believing that I just had to accept that life was going to be awesome and wasn't going to suck.

I boarded a plane for Dallas for school two days after my grandfather's funeral. And while reading on the plane, a thought struck my heart and a new mentality was born. It was in that moment that I figured out that it was okay to accept that, indeed, life is like an elevator. But although life is like an elevator, your mind doesn't necessarily have to be.

We can't control everything that happens in life, but we can control what we do during life. And that even means that you can change the thoughts that run through the mind. However, what's not always said is that mind state is a choice. If you leave your mind to react as the world sees fit, the mind will be like the elevator with many highs and many lows. But when you decide that your mind is only going to go in one direction and one direction only, it becomes like an escalator.

When you get on an escalator, it only goes one direction, either up or down. That is the exact reason why you have to master the power of your mind and thoughts. When you take 100% control of your thoughts, you now decide when you are going to elevate and when you want to come down. This isn't an easy mentality to grasp for a person with a weak mind. This takes time to achieve for many. But the good news is, it's doable. None of what I've said to you is false. It can be done and I'm living proof that it's possible. Taking control of the mind means a mastery of emotional intelligence and taming the subconscious. That can only be done through constant practice and commitment to being aware of your thoughts and emotions. It's my belief that the world around you will come to its knees for you if you truly believe that it's your time to get what's owed to you.

**What's Going On In Your Head?**

There has never been a storm on this Earth as bad as the storm that occurs in a chaotic mind. A mind in chaos sees a calamitous world even in the most beautiful environments. The climate of your mind has a lot to do with your moral compass. When a person goes into a negative place, his or her words change. Some will hurt people and not even know they are doing it. Whether through words or acts, chaos in the mind leads us in the wrong direction. But we are in a place to grow from all of this.

When we take sole responsibility of governing ourselves down to the minds, we will see an elevation in altitude in our lives. Let's talk through some of the benefits of having a peaceful mind:

- Clearer Vision: It becomes easier to see the bigger picture.
- Focus: You can sharpen your focus and identify what needs to be done to "make moves".

- Fewer Distractions: When your mind is at peace, you have fewer distractions. There is also less room for regret.
- Love Better: It's easier to show love and enjoy the blessings that life has to offer.
- Confidence Spike: When your mind is clear, it becomes much easier to walk around with your head held high.

Now to the average person who's "got their life together" this probably sounds like nothing. Well, let me be the first to tell you that there are people in this world that will take you out of it for a shot at that kind of peace. Build the Escalator Complex to where your mind believes that the only direction you are worthy of is up.

**Practice Makes Perfect**

*Replica championships rings are easy to acquire. To become the champion requires work.*

No champion just wakes up with a ring. Rings are earned through hard work and consistency. You have to build daily practices that **result in rings**. It's really that simple. Let's look at some of the techniques that you could use to build a stronger mind state.

**Writing it Out**

Let me be very vocal about this: I am #TeamWriter. I'm all about writing out your thoughts. I actually got this style of clearing the mind from Army Officer Brigadier General Charles Masaracchia. When he was my commander, he used to push out an email on weekends that he called his "Random Thoughts". In this email, it was literally his reflections on how our unit's week went and what we needed to do to grow as people and as a unit. That style of reflection changed the way that I saw life forever. Everyday, I sit down and write out how my day went and how I can improve the next day. In fact, while writing my random thoughts out, I even write down funny and positive moments that happened during my day like the cleaning lady giving me a huge smile as she took out my trash. These may seem minute and irrelevant, but trust me, after a 4am wake up, getting yelled at during the day, a 10-mile run, and putting out fires all day, you'll be searching for positive vibes. Trust me. But all jokes aside, this is a great opportunity to dump out everything on your mind, down to the situations that are keeping you up at night. I've come to learn that no matter how big a situation may seem, once you place it on paper, it immediately loses its power because now it's in front of your face for you to confront.

**Workouts**

There is no feeling like a body after a workout. Your stress decreases, brain functionality improves, and confidence radiates.

**Shrink the Issue**

You ever heard of making a mountain out of a molehill? Yeah, we have the tendency to that at times. Sometimes, all we have to do is step back and look at a situation and the answer will be right under our noses. However, when we are literally in the fight, everything seems worse than it really is. We have to get out of that mindset that if it's a problem, to elevate it to being the worst catastrophe to hit mankind. It's not. It's just another problem that needs fixing. The more power you give to a situation, the stronger it becomes. Take away the power from your situations and watch it become so much easier to eliminate your challenges.

**Show Gratitude**

Understand that not everyone in the world can deal with the challenge that you're currently facing, so be thankful you were deemed capable of handling this challenge. Like it's said in Bible, you will not have more placed on you than you can bare. So celebrate having this much weight placed on you. You are deemed capable of getting the job done. Prove yourself right.

**Meditation**

Before I start this one off, let me say I am not a Yogi. But I do know that there is peace to be found in meditation. I recently started meditating after my morning workouts. I use it as an opportunity to absorb the positive energy of everything around me.

**Sitting in Silence**

Most of the time in chaos, the mind is moving at 100 miles per hour. Sometimes, it's even moving beyond that speed. But it's important to note that when the mind is thinking of a million things, sometimes the wisest move to make is none; literally. Maybe it's time to take a moment to welcome silence. In the midst of silence, the brain is capable of pausing everything crazy occurring around it. Think of silence as your reset button. In silence, nothing is happening and nothing exists. It's just you in the moment. This is your chance to cancel out everything happening in the world and to just enjoy momentary bliss.

In college, I spread myself way too thin. There was a time where I held six leadership positions while working on school and becoming an Army officer. I was super overwhelmed and never had the heart to tell anyone. In fact, this is the first time I have ever told anyone how stressed I was during that time. In fact, I found myself doing so much that I eventually stopped gaining results. I just became a walking responsibility rather than a leader who could help those around him. It felt like no matter how good life became, the achievements I made, or the rewards I received, I could never truly get my legs beneath me. I was always heading to meeting. On weekends, I was heading to a conference or an event to show support or to contribute. Weekends that I could've spent just being a college student were spent in bed due to a lack of energy. In fact, I've even had days where even when I had nothing going on, I would just walk campus because I felt like I should be doing something or something was coming that I wasn't expecting.

I lost touch with reality. I became the guy who would smile in a room of his peers but could've screamed for help because I was a lost soul with multiple leadership titles. Then one day, I just got fed up and couldn't take it anymore. I needed to save "me" from "myself". It was a Friday around three in the afternoon. Classes were done for the week and I had two meetings in the evening to attend for an upcoming on campus event. While walking out of a class, I could literally feel that I was inches away from snapping. I felt like nothing around me mattered. The grades were a system's assessment that would be obsolete the day I graduated. The positions I held would be irrelevant just a few weeks after graduation. Not to mention, walking into a room of people that you knew couldn't stand you doesn't mean you have to be fake-loving towards them to get things done. In that moment when all of those thoughts began to hit, the way I saw the world began to change.

I called the chairmen for both meetings and declined making the meetings. When asked why I wasn't coming, they both got the same response, "I'm about to have a mental breakdown and all of you are why". I then ran to my dorm room and changed out of my suit and tie into jogging pants, a tan Army t-shirt, shades, and a fitted hat. I rushed out to my car and hit the road for Fort Bragg, North Carolina. I drove out to our normal training site for my ROTC group. Once I arrived, I parked my car and went about three miles into the woods with a tent built for one and a sleeping bag.

I pulled out a cigarette, lit it, and sat in pure silence while the sun went down. That moment was one of the greatest that I had ever experienced in my life. The world stood still, there were no reports to do, and no one was in my face evaluating my appearance and actions. From that night in the woods, I found out that it was okay to just be by yourself. The silence helped me clear my mind, appreciate my surroundings, and refocus on what really mattered in my life. So, if you're looking to clear the canvas of your life before you take another step, you're in control. As much as they tell you they can't wait, guess what? Yes, they can and you have the power to make them wait while you prepare yourself to give the world the best you. Take solace in self in silence and then come back ready to be the best "<Insert Your Name> 2.0".

## Counseling

Sometimes it's hard to move forward because everything behind you is holding you back. Do you understand that holding on to whatever hurt you in the past could extend the time it takes you to become the greatest edition of you by days, months, years, and even decades? Where's the X-Box…because someone thinks this is a game. Well, let me tell you, I'm not joking around with you right now. It's important to eliminate as much dead weight as possible when you've accepted that there's something bigger out there for you. Proverbs 11:14 says, *"Where there is no guidance, a people falls, but in an abundance of counselors, there is safety."*

---

*If your mind is not 100% at peace, that is a mental health issue; no matter how small!!!!*

---

I want you to truly understand that. Mental health issues can be acute and/or chronic. There are lot of people who believe that they don't have mental issues if they are not suicidal, depressed, or something of these magnitudes. Stop telling false truths. In a moment of stress, the mind isn't normal, therefore it is a temporary mental issue that can be fixed by eliminating the stress.

But to stay on topic, there's no shame in seeking counseling. However, the counsel you seek needs to be wise. **Seek foolish counsel, expect foolish results. Seek**

**wise counsel, expect to become wiser.** Seek someone who has been where you've been before. It's seeking out someone who has gone through your pain and latching on to them for advice and growth. Consider seeking counseling as acquiring a "mental growth coach". They are giving you the tools you need to defeat the mental adversaries in your life. Normally, the people who claim they don't need help need the most out of everybody.

My father's name was Ken; just like me. I didn't know my father until I was six years old. On top of that at the tender age of six, my father committed suicide five days after I met him. After my father's death, I went to his funeral and can only remember all of the people telling me how great of a man my father was. So I worked to make him proud based on all the superlatives people told me he was. I walked around everyday with a smile on my face and operating normally with no one knowing the chaos in my mind.

I spent the next two decades just trying to figure out who my father was. In fact, I spent so much of my life trying to be like my dad, that I was eventually 28 and realized that I was living my life for a man who I didn't even know that well. I made a false image of who my dad was. I made him perfect. He was wise, kind, athletic, an awesome speaker, a leader, a loyal friend, and so much more.

You could imagine the mental effect it had on me once I realized that I was trying so hard to be someone I was not and create someone who wasn't. I felt for a little while like I was trying to live someone else's life. I was walking around with the stress of not being on his level, pressure of not meeting his image, and failing to be that great. But when the day came and I awoke from my personally-woven lies, I realized that I needed to take my life back and become Ken Coleman rather than Ken Ruffin. When I realized my predicament, I accepted that I didn't know how to this fix this and even if I did, I couldn't get out of this chaos alone. I needed someone who would walk into the fire and bring me out alive. I immediately sought counseling to let go of the pain and disappointment.

What I eventually found out was, I had always been myself. This guy who was kind, loving, approachable, professional, a leader, and more was all in me. I gave my dad the characteristics that I already possessed or desired. What I was really feeling was the disappointment of not having a dad, going to family events without my dad, missing out on those father-son moments, and more. The biggest thing I found was that I was upset that I became the stereotype of being another fatherless black kid. I didn't come to grips with these demons until I was 28. And I can confidently say, these demons would still follow me to this day if I didn't seek counseling.

**What Makes You Think the Way You Do?**

What you do on a daily basis in rhythm like clockwork can be referred to as a habit. What you do on a daily basis is also who you truly are. Therefore, if you'd like to see the definition of a person, check their habits. I think it's important to take the time to look at what make us tick. If you know what makes you tick, you can control your surroundings better. There are people who walk around with daily routines and habits that they've never taken time to assess.

Like really, have you ever just taken time to look at 24 hours in your day and say "Why do I do what I do?" What's funny is that if you look deep enough, you'll start finding out that you've got more time than you think and you've just been wasting it. You'll find out that some of your habits don't help you grow, yet you do them almost religiously. You'll find that what you desire but haven't achieved is because the direction you're going in doesn't lead to your desired destination.

Reflecting on my habits started to matter more to me after my grandfather passed away. The doctor partially blamed the cause of his passing on an excess use of salts in his diet. What I began to wonder was if you begin to develop medical issues related to something that you can change, why don't you just change them? After his passing, I made a promise to myself again that if I saw a change in the way my body was working, I'd immediately contact a doctor to fix it. Why? Because even the act of moving slow to resolve issues is a habit.

I had the desire to become a professional speaker who spoke intelligently but could still keep it real in any room I walked into. After taking inventory of myself, I found that some of my habits weren't helping me. I had to reduce the amount of cursing I was exposed to. While listening to a speech by the late Dr. Myles Munroe, I noted that he harped on the power of having a command over your language. I found myself walking around and having conversations with people talking like the music I heard knowing that wasn't how I desired to speak. As soon as I replaced my music with clean content and podcasts, I began to see changes in my tongue.

I also wanted to get myself back into shape. With my previous routine, I was waking up at 3am to be at the gym by 6am. Then I would go to the gym and just pick machines based on how I felt that day. On top of that, I was still eating how I wanted. I eventually realized that I was getting older and couldn't eat a pizza Monday night and run like a gazelle on Tuesday anymore. To fix my habits, I gave myself back two hours of sleep. I wasn't getting enough sleep to function during the day nor was I recovering from my previous brutal day. I also changed out all of my snacks. I ate just as much as I did previously, but it was just healthier foods. With this one change, I went from 225 to 202lbs in six months and I'm still going.

Now, everyone is going to have habit challenges. Some people can manage a bountiful life and still continue to keep every habit that I've substituted. But if you are someone who believes that there is a way to elevate your life, the answer of how to change from minimal to monumental growth could be in a simple change of habits. Note, I didn't tell you to get rid of anything. What I did was substitute what I was previously doing for a choice that was better for my growth.

When your mind is strong, your ability to improve your life grows exponentially. But you've got to commit to building healthy habits and slowly making changes will build the best version of you that you desire. At the end of the day, you are a reflection of your soul. You can hide from anybody in this world except for you. You can look as pretty as you wish and dress as nicely as you want, but if your mind is in dismay and lacks peace, you'll never be at your best or even able to reach it. And even if you make it to the end, you will still have delayed the time it would've taken you to win. Trust me when I say this: Master the mind and the rest will fall into place. There's a reason for the phrase "Mind Over Matter".

# DOPE Exercise 5: Letter to Someone I Love

On a separate sheet of paper, I want you to write a letter to someone special in your life about why you will (continue to) seek mental peace. Whether you're speaking to a parent, boy/girlfriend, wife/husband, ex, even a child, take this letter and write it with conviction. In fact, I left one person out. If you aren't going to write to someone else, write to yourself. I'm going to give you some genuine example statements from me. At a minimum, you need to write about the following:

- Date: That's your timestamp of the day you committed to changing your life for the better.
- Purpose of the Letter: For example, "Dear children, Daddy is writing to you while you're still very young to tell you I'm investing in my mental health".
- Why You're Investing in Your Mind: For example, "I'm doing this because you deserve a daddy who cares for himself so he can care for you. You deserve someone who can love you better than my parents did me".
- How You're Going About Seeking a more Powerful Mind: For example, "I'm getting mental counseling from psychiatrists, I've hired a life coach, I've changed what I'm feeding my spirit, and I'm playing with you twice as much now so I can find even more reasons to fall in love with you".

- Are You Ashamed: For example, "I was ashamed when I started this journey. I didn't want to get help but I knew that I'd be better if I got help. So I'm doing this".

Promise Not to Give up: For example, "I promise not to give up. I will continue to work on my mindset daily. This is a daily journey and folding under pressure isn't in our bloodline".

# Chapter Six:
# The Body of Work

With every stab of a pick into the arm of the icy giant, we felt something different. We felt power, hope, focus, will, and so many other emotions. This was it. We were at the end of the road. With tired muscles and drained minds, we continued to progress. In this moment, I began to reflect on everything. I thought about having to turn away people who lacked discipline even though they were good people. I thought of hearing the complaints of teammates yet continuing to walk. I remembered pulling Lex in and turning him into a leader. I remember going through some of the worst moments of my life. On the side of this mountain, I revisited my demons and made acquaintance with new ones before slaying them. I reflected as much as possible to keep my focus. And then, the most inspiring moment of our trip hit us.

We finally saw the sun peaking over the mountain. It was amazing to look and see that. We were so close to solidifying our legacy. This was our chance to leave our mark on this Earth and we were not to be denied. Before I got the chance to scream out to the team to keep going, I heard Lex let out an inspirational outcry, "THIS IS IT! WE ARE SO CLOSE! LET'S GOOOOO!"

You could feel the blood begin to warm, the heart began to beat with authority, and the eyes began to perk up. We knew this was it, we were there. *Click Clack,*

*Click, Clack.* That was the sound of our icepicks drilling into the mountain with sheer determination. *Click, Clack, Click, Clack.* We were feet away from reaching our dream. We knew if we just held on and kept moving, we would make it.

This was the moment where the late nights in the gym, studying climbing and belay techniques, and more would come into play. It all culminated for this one moment. The moment where we were thousands of feet in the air hanging on by a thread. Our mental had been tested by cold and fatigue. Our souls had been tested by the rigorous terrain. This was definitely it. The body of work mattered in this moment... right now.

30 feet out... 25 feet... 20 feet... 15 feet...10 feet...5 feet...

I reached my hand up and climbed on top of the peak. Once I climbed up, without haste, I turned and grabbed my teammates, one by one ensuring their safety onto the frozen flat surface. Once everyone had made it to the top of the ice, we looked around us. We had made it to the top of Mount Altitude. It was surreal. As the team began to celebrate being on top of the mountain, on top of life, and on top of the world; I reflected on what we had gone through to get here.

**Sacrifices Must Be Made**

In taking the road less traveled, sacrifices must be made. This may mean more late nights and early mornings. It could mean extra laps around the track or pool. It may even mean cutting people off as you begin to win. But where changes need to be made, you have to be willing to make them. To get to the next level, there are some beloved people that you may have to walk away from forever just because this dream matters more. You can see the future and they can only see Saturday.

Now, I'm going to speak to you from the heart. This isn't an easy thing to do. Giving up people and actions will hurt in the worst way. But these are wounds that heal. In fact, you may even find your willingness to change could spark the change in a friend who looks up to you.

When graduating high school, I decided to make some major changes in my life that would shake the very fabric of my existence. I chose suits and ties over my white tees and baggy jeans. I chose to stop fake gang banging and put the bandanas away. I chose college over running the streets. I chose books and the Army over pushing marijuana and cocaine. I left my city in hopes of living a better life. I almost feel as if I chose life over death. But it came with a hard price.

When I came home, it tore me apart to see the people I once hung with. Many people seemed to be falling deeper into the abyss called ghetto life. And Wilson, North Carolina isn't even a ghetto, but young black men and women were walking around as if it was. My grandparents lived right up the road from local drug dealers. The crazy thing was I used to go to church with some of those guys so it blew me away to see them on the corner dealing. I visited the community center where I used to play basketball and dance. It was like a ghost town in there.

No one was playing ball, it was just silence. I almost wondered for a moment if the city forgot about these young black kids and they, in turn, responded by heading to the streets. Some of my closest friends had died in drunk driving accidents or shootouts as certain areas of the city started becoming worse. I even saw adults who used to come to my house to visit my grandparents strung out on coke at the local gas stations asking me for money.

And as crazy as this may sound, I felt as if I was part of the problem. I felt like I failed my city because I left. I felt as if I left the brothers and sisters who needed me. But I am grateful because I could've been them. Then, how could I help to bring motivation to them and the next generation of children? Traveling the road that took me away from home hurt. But being the man I am now was worth walking away, because the man I am now can contribute to positive change rather just be another complainer.

Sometimes to grow, something has to go. I'm not asking you to sacrifice your soul. I'm just asking you to eliminate what will interfere with you fulfilling your ultimate purpose. Don't allow poor relationships to destroy your future. It's happened to many men and you can fall victim as well if you allow yourself to. In life, no matter what, take the road less traveled. The road less traveled will always culminate in the greatest you at the highest altitude possible.

**Your Work Will Always Be Tested**

One of my favorite movies of all time is "I Think I Love My Wife" starring Chris Rock and Kerry Washington. Kerry, who plays the gorgeous Nikki True (I'm so sure this was a Prince reference), says a line that has sat with me for years now. After meeting with her friend Richard after years, she asks him if he loves his wife. After he tells her yes, she responded with what was a life changing statement, *"No you don't, you didn't say it right. I hear ice cracking."* This merely means in Richard's case, his marriage isn't that strong and it could be breaking slowly right in front of his eyes. The bigger message to me was that she was able to look at him and felt the confidence to be able to question him, period. As the movie progressed she was proved to be correct as he continued to commit actions that a man in a solid marriage wouldn't make. However, in the end his love for wife and family prevailed, thus deterring him from taking Nikki's advances.

The real reason his marriage was beginning to break was because he was allowing it to break. His wife was walking around with the picture that their marriage was okay even though there wasn't a lot happening in their bedroom. Richard, from the beginning of the movie, talked about how boring his marriage was. The truth was the marriage was boring because he didn't put in the work to make it interesting. This is a textbook example of what happens when you fail to put in a body of work.

Your body of work and willingness to sacrifice will always determine your growth. To make it clear, there will always be a price associated with growth. No matter whether we're talking about relationships, bank accounts, notoriety, there will always be a price. There is no gain without sacrifice. I mean, even to gain death, you have to sacrifice life. In my $5^{th}$ grade science class, my teacher taught me that energy can't be destroyed; only transferred. That scientific law is one of the coolest things about us human beings. There is an unlimited supply of energy surrounding us that can be converted but never eliminated.

Women are born and within decades are capable of giving birth. We are capable of turning clay into bricks, steel into cars, and words into art. All of this is embedded in your DNA at birth. But each of these capabilities is based on how much energy you are willing to expound to get the job done. The transfer of energy can build empires. When you envision the transfer of energy, I want you to envision atoms flowing from the body into the air and building your dreams. There's a certain amount and type of energy that you have to give to manifest your desires.

**Consistency Increases Value In Life (CIVIL)**

I'm a huge football fan. But in particular right now, let's talk college football. With the introduction of the College Football Playoff system, teams are now assessed solely based on a body of work by a playoff committee. To the playoff committee, body of work means a lot of different things to include:

- Strength of Schedule
- Strength of Record
- +/- points per game
- Ranking
- What other loses/wins

When you apply for a job, what does a body of work look like?

- Key Words
- Experience
- Education

The key takeaway is that in everything you do, there is a body of work required and each of them requires the exact same thing: proven results and consistency. Are you consistently winning? Are you consistently seeking development? Do you consistently get the job accomplished? Are you consistently being placed in a position of leadership? That's why I came up with the acronym CIVIL. Because it is true that consistency increases value in life.

The more consistent you are, the more attractive you become in everything that you do. When people believe that passing the ball to you guarantees a win, you become an unstoppable force. When people believe in you and see you as a man or woman who is about creating leverage for the team by any means, you become the person that everyone has to have on their team. People begin to want to work for you. Even intimate relationships begin to change. I mean, who doesn't want to date a winner? I know I do. That's one of the reasons I'm with my wife.

### Stages of the Body of Work

**The Accountable Stage.** Consistency isn't made overnight. It's worked at on a daily basis, claimed, and then maintained over a lifetime. With every person that you meet, you'll always start off with being accountable. That means if you meet someone and you're starting at ground zero, all you get is however much trust they are willing to provide you upfront and confirmation that they are holding you accountable for everything you succeed or fail to do. To be honest with you, if they provide you trust up front, you should value it. That's very special. Not to mention people are willing to trust a stranger right off a street with a project, tasks, or even a friendship up front. It doesn't matter if you're working for a well-known company. In that instance, the average person trusts the brand and the logo, not the person talking to them. **So if you get free trust, guard it with your life.**

**The Execution Stage.** During the execution stage, people are evaluating your every move. They are assessing how you plan, communicate, make decisions, keep them in the loop, and how well you get the work done. This stage defines if your client, friend, or manager is going to continue to hand out trust. The scary part during this stage is that you don't know how much weight your individual mistakes will have. You could perform every other task correctly, but if you mess up one task in the particular (i.e. the sacred task) your relevancy is dead. For a company, it could be not requesting enough before funds shut off, forcing the company to operate in the red (yes, I've heard of this happening before). For a client, it could be promising to ship a product to them and the product doesn't make it when you guaranteed it. For a friend, it could be telling a secret that you swore to keep between the two of you. Fail to perform to standard and your body of work could mean nothing. So I'm confident with saying that the execution stage is the most sensitive stage of building relationships. If you execute well and get the results your teammate expected, then you'll gain their trust that you can get the job done.

**The Consistency Stage.** Once you enter the consistency stage, you've already proven that you are capable of getting things done. Now it's just about proving that you can repeat what you did in the execution stage over and over. Eventually, you'll move out of execution into the consistency stage. At this point, you now have the trust of your leadership, clients, peers, or subordinates. However, the work isn't done. In this phase you are now in a position to speak on situations related to whatever it is that you do. When your voice is being heard and advice you provide is being taken, it's safe to suspect you are approaching or have already entered this stage. Once you reach the consistency stage, your goal should be to not lose trust.

**Your Last 24 Hours**

No, I'm not going to ask a question about, "If you had 24 hours to live…" Those are old and played out now. On the contrary, let me tell you a little secret about your body of work:

---

*Your body of work is only good as your last 24 hours.*

---

That means the day you put the work in is the day that it's good for. Take a look at some of the stellar people in our society. Jon "Bones" Jones is easily one of the greatest MMA fighters of all time. But after being busted for illegal substances, his greatness will forever be questioned. General David Patreus was one of the greatest strategic minds in the history of the United States Army. He later went on to become the director of the Central Intelligence Agency (CIA). But his 37-year rise to power was cut short after an affair and providing classified materials to his mistress cost him everything he worked for. Paula Deen was loved by all races for her ability to cook delicious food with a hint of Southern Hospitality. But after being caught saying the N-word at her workplace, most of her publishing deals and endorsements were terminated.

All of these stories validate one fact. No matter how high you get in stature, no matter how much respect you garnish from your works in life, you can still be touched. We live in a digital age now. One tweet, Instagram photo, DM, or post can destroy the reputations and livelihood of men and women. It's important to be humble and guard your reputation closely. I'm not telling you to walk around and be perfect because that's never going to happen. I am telling you, however, to be cautious of the moves you make. Life is for people who play chess. The man who plays the games using checker tactics will be removed from the table.

**Stay Away from Stagnancy**

Stagnancy has cost the birth of lives, inventions, and discussion that could have elevated human advancement. I understand that we as people need rest, but don't allow yourself to become lethargic. What happens when you don't go to gym after a long period of time and eat what you want? You start gaining weight, right? I know I'm right because I've been that guy in the past. Like I said earlier, you're only as good as your last 24 hours. You can't rest on the past. You know rules are meant to be broken? Well, so are records. It only takes one newcomer to upstage you. Then you will find yourself trailing someone else. Trust me when I say it's always more fun to play "follow the leader" than "catch-up".

In college, I ran incredibly fast. In ROTC, I felt like no one could keep up with me. I was such a fast runner that I was requested to join the inaugural track team at my college. Whether on the track team or in ROTC, I was clearly the fastest man on the team. In fact, I nicknamed myself The Flash because I was feeling myself just that much. Not to mention The Flash was super cocky anyway so it felt like a purpose catch-all name: "K-Cole The Flash".

Then one day we had a transfer student come in to the university. As soon he arrived to the school, he connected with our coach and requested to join the team. Since this was our inaugural team and we didn't plan on competing in conference play until the following year, he was immediately allowed to join. On a normal day, we had practice. He showed up in full track gear while the rest of us showed up in our shorts and tank tops. The entire team introduced themselves to him and welcomed him to the squad.

As the leader, I felt like I had to bring him in properly and set the standard that I was captain of this team and I expected him to give it all he had. Now normally during practice sprints, I would try to run just a little faster than the team for motivation purposes to make everyone step their game up. I was planning on doing the same thing with him, too. But evidently, he had other plans.

We got into position and eyed the finish line together. I stared him dead into his eyes as I always do my opponents to try to instill a little fear into him. But that day, I was the one instilled with fear because when I turned to look at him, he was already looking at me with a straight face and a smirk. As soon as the whistle went off, I looked straight ahead and ran at full speed. Nothing mattered in that moment but obliterating his confidence and morale. I planned to destroy him then build him back up. I ran and ran and ran. But before I knew it, he was at least 10 feet ahead of me and embarrassing me.

Needless to say, he beat me through the finish line. As I stopped to catch my breath, he walked up with little sweat and breathing normally carrying on regular conversations. I was in shock and embarrassed. But I wasn't embarrassed because I lost. It was because I saw the faces on my teammates and I knew that the passing of the torch had just occurred. However, it didn't happen because I lost; it was because I didn't control my emotions and made it clear that it was more about me than the team. My reputation of being a team-oriented athlete was destroyed on the spot and the team-focused superior athlete replaced me as team captain.

## Your Worth Should Match Your Work

I don't want to hear a man say he's millionaire material when he carries himself with an "I'm broke" mentality. That type of logic only flies in volcanoes and it's the same the place it dies. If you know your worth, the only challenge you have to deal with is communicating it to those around you. It's hard to communicate who you are in a short timeframe. That's why, going back to the previous sub section, you want your reputation to proceed you. If your previous work validates that you are the best at what you do, it takes less time to earn respect and develop rapport with new people.

You can't control how people see you, but you can definitely influence how you are perceived. Carry yourself like an executive and eventually executive privileges will appear. Carry yourself like you care about others and people will begin to care about you more. If you want to reach the next level, the doors are open. Walk in. But you better be ready to put in the work that comes with being at the level you think you deserve.

Being declared as a leader worthy of the next level isn't solidified when you get the position. It's solidified while you're in the trenches. When you're getting your hands dirty, people can make a pretty solid assessment of whether you can lead or not. In the Army, I've seen junior soldiers lead better than me. I'm not ashamed to admit that because credit should be given where it's due.

In order to reach the next height in altitude, you've got to be willing to put in the hours. There is no free ride on your way to the top of this mountain called Altitude. You've got to do your homework, earn trust, build a pattern of consistency, and repeat. That simple formula builds bosses, immortalizes reputations, and wins championships. Many will try to reach the summit, but only a chosen few will get there. That means you've only got two options: Summit or Submit.

# Chapter Seven:
# The Top of The World

Making it to the top is no easy feat. It's a magical experience that everyone deserves to experience at some point in their lives. No one can feel the excitement and emotions that go through you when you arrive. There are new experiences at the top of every mountain that you climb in your life. There's a change in name. You become Olympian, Champion, CEO, Soldier, Legend, Iconic, Parent, Husband, Wife, and a combination of many other titles. There's one title I want to close this book with that I want to become. But first, let's talk about what happens when you're finally on top of the world.

**Make Time to Celebrate**

In confidence and with authority, we have just proven that we have what it takes to reach the top of this mountain. That means that if we've done it once, we can do it again. And rest assured, you can do it again. However, tomorrow is never promised so it's important to make time to celebrate the now. Make time to celebrate your major victories in life. If that means a party, an announcement to the world, spinning tires on your car, or just breaking into your happy dance, make time. Don't be programmed to believe that wins aren't to be celebrated. Coaches take Gatorade baths, champagne gets popped in the locker rooms, and confetti angels are made when the confetti falls to the coliseum floor.

There's time for you to lock-in on your goals and then there's times to celebrate. What's the point of working hard for something if you can't even pat yourself on the back once you get it? You might as well be an android if that's the case. At that point, you're just working to work. There's no true purpose behind any of the blood, sweat, and tears you've shed to get here.

Take time to think about everything you went through. Think about the times you were told "you can't". Reflect on when the doubters wrote you off. Think about the nights you cried because you hadn't achieved the mountain top. Think about how close you were to the top and fell short. Now look at all of those situations, smile, and walk away from them. Because now they have served their purpose. This is why I said, let the pain hit you head on. This is why I said it's okay to fail. Because all of that failure led to this moment. You sacrificed so much to get here. The least you can do for yourself is relish in the fact that, against all odds, you stand at the top of Mt. Olympus. You stand among the Gods and are prepared to have your named etched in stone and carved on the hearts of every man, woman, and child who is privileged to hear your story. Celebrate yourself, because no matter how much everyone else celebrates with you, no one can celebrate for you and like you.

**Be Yourself**

When you are at the top of your game and start to gain significant notoriety, people begin to place you in a box. In this box are their expectations of who you should be, what your value systems should look like, and what you should stand for. Let's keep it as real as it can be said. No one can tell you how to act during your ascension or once you ascend to the top of the world. You can take advisory into consideration but at the end of the day, take pride in holding the cards. Conduct yourself in accordance with your value system and not someone else's. In the words of Charlamagne tha God, "Imma need you to keep that same energy." Some people will tell you, "you should conduct yourself differently. You should have more respect for the gold. You do realize your new stature, right?"

Respond with, "YES, I do know my new stature. And I know who I was before I got here." Don't let anyone else's expectation of who they believe you should be change you. If you were humble and soft spoken with the heart of a lion, then you still be that person. If you weren't confident and only spoke loud when you felt the need, you still be that person. If you're cocky and slick with the tongue but you can back up why you're the best, talk that talk. Just understand that if you fall, we expect you to keep talking smack. No one is in a position to tell you how to move when you reach the top except mentors you designate. They didn't care how you moved when you were up and coming. So don't let them control you now.

You have to be your most authentic self. With over 7.6 billion human beings on this planet, there's only one of you, period. Be proud of that fact and let no one put you in a position to ignore that. Being yourself comes with higher confidence, respect, and peace. When you don't give yourself the option to be fake, you'll always live the realist life.

## Never Forget The ~~Little~~ People

Who comes up with these phrases?! First off, the only little people I know are the haters trying to block your shine. You should never forget the people who got you here. When someone loans to you, you are in debt to them unless they do something to void the debt. Therefore, if someone contributed to your success, give the credit they deserve. This doesn't mean they made you. At the end of the day, YOU MADE YOU. But, they did invest time, energy, and resources into you to see you win. In my thank you comments, you'll see that I went very detailed with thanking certain people who contributed to not only the creation of this book, but contributed to developing my mentality.

You've got to seriously look and see how people have helped you. It's easy to get to the top and feel like you did it all on your own. It's easy to start feeling like you were a one-person show. The truth is help came from every angle around you. When you give back gratitude to the people who were a blessing to you, I believe more blessings manifest themselves. This is part of "being faithful over a few". Being faithful over few means that you've proven you can be trusted with little and are ready for the increase in responsibility, resources, and blessings.

When I was going through my divorce with my first wife, I thought my life was shattering in front of my very eyes. I was tens of thousands of dollars in debt. My credit score had been destroyed. I was kicked out of my home on-post and had no where to go. And on top of that, I was kicked out two days before Christmas. I was having suicidal ideations and plotting just how to do it so I could make sure my grandparents got paid and lived peacefully the rest of their lives.

But in my lowest moment, there were people who had my back. There were even people I ignored who I had to find out later on in life had my best interests at heart. Remembering the people who helped get you where you are keeps you humble and at times of remembrance, keeps you hungry. When you reflect during your gratitude time, you'll notice that some of those special moments you hold dear with those people become part of your "Why". They become part of your why do I wake up? Why do I put in these crazy hours? When I feel like giving up, why I continue to do this.

**Defend When Challenged**

In the UFC, nothing excites me more than to hear Bruce Buffer announce the arrival of the

> *"REIGNING, DEFENDING, UNDISPUTED CHAMPION OF THE WORLD!"*

As a champion, you are expected to defend the spot you earned at all times. When you climb to the top of the mountains in your life, the journey doesn't end. You now have to become a deeper student of your craft. I need you to master the game. The greatest championship victories normally come during the title defense. You've climbed to the top once. But can you do it again? New challenges the size of mountains will oppose you . But the good news is you've been here before.

You know what facing the ultimate opposition looks like. It's tall, daunting, and looks impossible. But it only looks impossible to those who have never completed the impossible. Defend your title every single day. Don't wait for the world to challenge you for the gold. You challenge the challengers. That keeps you fresh. It keeps you on your toes and ready for war when true tests show their heads.

In 2017, I suffered a back injury that shattered my confidence as a man. It just seemed like the world was coming down. And on top of that, the injury happened just as I recommitted myself to Crossfit and getting back into top physical condition. I was done and a comeback was pretty much impossible. But after I cried and got past my little feelings, I re-focused.

I remembered who I was. I was the guy who lost his home, lost his family, found out he was raising a kid that wasn't his, had lost his dream job, and had two children with speech delay and heart disease. With all that going on in my life, I couldn't give up. I had people counting on me to win. Not to mention in this moment, suicide couldn't be the answer. I couldn't do what my father did. That's just asking for a generational curse and the start of a vicious cycle. It was time to start a new way of living.

So I chose to stand as the champion and not as the victim. I asked life to come at me head on. And as it got colder in elevation, I climbed. As avalanches occurred, I watched it pour, unafraid, and chose a new route no matter how challenging because I wouldn't be denied. As people left out of my life and told me I was no one, stabbed me in the back, and prayed for my downfall, I drove my pick into the ice and I climb with every ounce of belief I had left in my body. As the pains of physical therapy made it difficult to walk and recover, I declared that I would never be denied.

And on April 12, 2018, I was cleared to lead a normal life again with no regrets, no surgeries, and no looking back. That moment was the culminating event in my life and re-affirmed to me that I can survive anything that comes my way. I don't fear life. Life should fear me. I can't be deterred. No matter how many demons cross my path, I will slay them all one-by-one and I expect the exact same from you. You weren't built to beg for mercy. You were built to deliver it when needed. So defend your throne with all of your might until the end of time.

**My Final Request to You**

There are young men and women starving for leadership and only you can fill that void. Who better to teach the youth of this nation how to achieve their dreams than someone who has done it? You owe you and I understand that, but I beg you to make time to sew into someone else. Your mentorship on how to survive, ride a bike, do math, manage a bank account, and more can do wonders in this world. The best part is that since you have seen the top of the mountain, they will trust you and believe in you.

Please don't leave the youth of this world hanging at a time where society is destroying our sons and daughters. You are needed and your guidance is crucial to ending foolish cycles of divide, struggle, and pain. Every single one of us has power and we can make society better if we are willing to come down from our heights in altitude to bring someone else up there with us. The reason I told you to celebrate, remain you, and be ready to defend your ascension at all times is because they need to know it can be done.

They need to know that I can be myself and still bring about change. They need to know that in their hands lie the evolution that will grow and unify borders, bandage damaged relationships, and welcome in a new generation of young leaders. I can tell you what happens when leaders who have made it don't decide to mentor once they make it to the top.

This is my most memorable military experience ever, so I felt it only right to hold this to the end to express the importance of mentoring someone. As a recently commissioned Second Lieutenant, I arrived in South Korea with only $15 to my name. In fact, I went three days with no food in my beautiful hotel room in the Dragon Hill Lodge in Seoul, South Korea. I let my frat brother, 1SG Charles Tyson, know I was in town and he immediately came to the hotel.

I didn't tell him my money situation because I felt uncomfortable. He was a First Sergeant and I was an Officer. There's this false stigma in the Army that Officers should always be smarter and capable of managing situations better than our non-commissioned officer (Sergeant) counterparts. But he took me out to eat, on him, and took time to coach me on how Korea works, cool places to go and do, and so forth.

On the fourth day, my bus finally arrived to take me to my new unit. Once I arrived, I went in to the Battalion and let out a sigh of relief. My new boss was a Captain and a young one at that, in his late 20s- early 30s. I felt like I had this in the bag and would get the coaching and development I needed to become better and most importantly, have someone to teach me how to master a bank account.

My first week in uniform at my unit, I arrived ready to get to work. I arrived during a busy period as we were preparing for major military exercises within the next two months. Each of the companies in my battalion were scattered throughout South Korea. During this week, my Captain decided to go and visit one of the companies at Camp Humphrey in Pyeongtaek.

After the visit to the company, the ride back was fairly quiet. In our van, there was my Captain, our Staff Sergeant who was driving, me, and two senior Sergeants. I felt that with a vehicle full of seasoned professionals, this could be the perfect place to get advice on how to grow financially before we got back to the office and eventually back to business. The response I've received back from them is still, to this day, the most embarrassing response I've ever received from someone.

I asked my question, "Hey, everybody. I need some advice. I'm not really good with my money. In fact when I came to Korea, I came here with a little under $20 in my pocket and I still don't know how to manage a budget account that well. Can anyone here tell me the best way to manage money?" Now, I know this question was very vague but I knew it would clearly get across what I was looking for. Here's the response I received from the Captain along with every Sergeant in the car that day: "HAHAHAHAHAHAHAHAHAHAHAHAHAHA!!!!!! YOU'RE AN OFFICER! YOU BETTER FIGURE IT OUT OR YOU'LL GO BROKE!"

All of them laughed, almost in unison, at me and I couldn't believe it. That was the day the Captain lost me. I didn't follow him because I had to. I followed him because the rank required me to do so. It was in that moment, I said to myself inside that I would never let another day go by where I wasn't trying to mentor or grow someone around me. The day I stop trying to grow the people around me is the day that I have left this world.

I'm asking you to join this commitment with me. Yes, you have climbed high in Altitude, but there is a higher level that you can manifest with your life experiences. And that's coaching and teaching someone else how to climb higher than you. You can get them to your level and help them go higher. You can impose upon them your successes and failures as I have done for you with this book. You remained a master of your craft so you could produce the masters that would propel this world long after your physical body is gone and your soul becomes the energy that guides the men and women into the future.

No matter what you do, continue the climb. Teach someone how to climb. Teach someone else how to be resilient. And before you know it, everyone will be climbing to a better place, a better reality, and a better tomorrow. Together.

## ELEVATE IN ALTITUDE FOREVER!

# About the Author

Ken "K. Fitz" Coleman's brand is defined in one word: Leadership. He prides himself on his ability to lead with compassion, develop leaders to one day take his place, and create a culture of belonging. Ken is committed to developing his community through service initiatives that promote unity and belonging.

Ken graduated from Fayetteville State University with a Bachelor of Arts in Political Science and Government and is currently pursuing his MBA. In addition, he is a career military man proudly serving in the United States Army.

## Connect with the Author

**Website:** www.officialkfitz.com

**Facebook:** @officialkfitz

**Instagram:** @officialkfitz

**Twitter:** @officialkfitz

**Anchor:** anchor.fm/officialkfitz

**YouTube:** Dream Mover TV

Don't forget to stream the "Altitude Podcast" on all major podcast platforms.

## Creative Control With Self-Publishing

**Divine Legacy Publishing provides authors with the guid-ance necessary to take creative control of their work through self-publishing. We provide:**

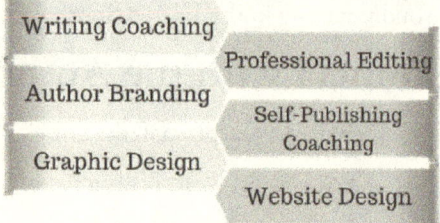

**Let Divine Legacy Publishing help you master the business of self-publishing.**

www.ingramcontent.com/pod-product-compliance
Lightning Source LLC
Chambersburg PA
CBHW031403040426
42444CB00005B/395